Stuart and
Cromwellian
Foreign
Policy

MODERN BRITISH FOREIGN POLICY

General Editor: MALCOLM ROBINSON
Head of the History Department, Radley College

Tudor Foreign Policy   P. S. CROWSON
Stuart and Cromwellian Foreign Policy   G. M. D. HOWAT

In preparation
The Eighteenth Century   P. LANGFORD
The Nineteenth Century   P. M. HAYES
The Twentieth Century   P. M. HAYES

By the same author
Fom Chatham to Churchill (1966)
(with Anne Howat) The Story of Health (1967)
(ed.) Dictionary of World History (1973)
Documents in European History, 1789–1970 (1973)

MODERN BRITISH FOREIGN POLICY

Stuart and Cromwellian Foreign Policy

G. M. D. Howat

ST. MARTIN'S PRESS
NEW YORK

For my daughter, Gillian

Contents

Foreword

The chronological limits of this book are 1603 to 1688, the period between the accession of James I and the departure of James II eighty-five years later. There is a case for considering the twenty-six years which followed: William III had Stuart blood, a Stuart wife and was succeeded by a Stuart queen. All are embraced in Sir George Clark's volume, *The Later Stuarts*, in the Oxford History of England. But in the context of foreign policy, 1688 is a reasonable date at which to end a survey, since the policies of William III and Anne are more in line with those of the eighteenth century. In so far as William pursued English objectives—as opposed to Dutch ones—he pursued those which were equally well sustained in the War of the Spanish Succession, the War of the Austrian Succession, the Seven Years War and, indeed, right up to the Congress of Vienna in 1815.

The geographical limits one should impose after 1603 are less clear. The kings of England were kings of Great Britain, but their policies were essentially English. It was only Oliver Cromwell who attempted a broad-based British foreign policy. Scotland, from whence the Stuarts came, had its own parliament, but it never presented those monarchs with a direct confrontation over foreign policy, although William III faced one when the Scottish Darien enterprise conflicted with his Spanish policy. That Scots incursion represented the beginnings of a trade revival, which expanded after the Union of 1707; had it been more evident in the seventeenth century as a whole, the Scots might have made a bigger impact upon the policies followed up to 1688.

The policies pursued by the crown—or the Protectorate—also embraced Ireland and Wales, since neither enjoyed a legislative independence parallel to that of Scotland. Whether those policies pleased Irishmen and Welshmen is another matter. Many Irish had close links with both Spain and France, whose Catholicism was often at variance with English Protestantism. On the other hand, the Welsh in the seventeenth century were often identified with English interests: the squirearchy supported the royalists; puritanism appealed to some; and there was a certain amount of Anglo-Welsh intermarriage.

English foreign policy was conducted in relation to events in Europe. The word 'Europe' itself is more comfortably used by a geographer than an historian, for whom it becomes a linguistic convenience which had less meaning in the seventeenth century than in the Middle Ages. For Europe represented kingdoms and republics, sovereignty and subjection, unitary government and federation, town and country, seafaring Scandinavians and land-locked Germans, priest and pastor. It was the continent of far-flung Norway, on whom the Renaissance made little impact, and of the capital of France, where literature, drama, art and music set cultural standards for others to envy.

Towards this diversified Europe looked the Stuart kings and Cromwell. If they looked further afield—to the East and to the Americas—they did so because colonies were a projection of the European interest. Colonial aspirations led the European nations to measure each other up in terms of trade.

Some decisions of a policy-nature call for comment. Quotations have not been footnoted. In almost every case, passages in inverted commas represent the original dialogue of a speech, treaty, report, pamphlet or letter of the times. A bibliography provides a selective list of books published since 1900 on the seventeenth century. As much as possible I have followed modern usage in limiting the number of capital letters used in describing offices, ranks and institutions. The adjective 'Imperial', with a capital, refers to the Holy Roman Empire.

This book was written during the months when Britain was participating in the last stages of the negotiations which in 1973 brought her into the European Economic Community. The member nations laid aside the historic feuds which had bedevilled their relations for generations. A book on seventeenth-century foreign policy must examine those European conflicts. Whether or not we learn from history—the great debate—we should recognize the fact that the divided Europe of the past has at last given way to the unified Europe of the 1970s. As we welcome peace, so we rejoice.

I have been lucky enough to have this book read while in preparation by two friends and scholars whose judgements I have respected and usually obeyed, Leonard Naylor and Malcolm Robinson. I am most grateful to both of them.

North Moreton   GERALD HOWAT
Berkshire
   May 1973.

1 The foreign policy of the nation, 1603–88

'For my name and memory, I leave it to men's charitable speeches and to foreign nations, and the next ages'

Francis Bacon

There is a purpose in the foreign policies of the sixteenth and eighteenth centuries which is lacking in those of the seventeenth. It was the business of the Tudors to secure a dynasty and of the Hanoverians to sustain an empire. The Tudor dynasty was secured when Spanish threats were offset: by the end of Elizabeth I's reign only the lack of an heir made necessary a graceful concession to the House of Stuart. But no upstarts, pretenders or alternative princesses toppled Henry VII, his son or his grandchildren.

The Hanoverians, at the hands of Walpole, the Pitts and Liverpool, matched the French in trade or in war, both in Europe and overseas. By 1763 England enjoyed a position of economic and political strength which included surveillance of the North American continent and the West Indies. The image was dimmed in 1783 when the thirteen colonies were lost, but by 1815 the defeat of Napoleon renewed domestic confidence in the nation, its constitution and its colonies. In the hour of victory uncomfortable questions about the trusteeship of empire and the social conditions of England could be put on one side; an empire had been sustained.

No such clarity of purpose can be found in the foreign policy of the seventeenth century. There is a lack of common ground in the respective intentions of the early Stuarts, Oliver Cromwell and the later Stuarts. There is no consistent and widely accepted historic enemy, such as the Spanish during the second half of the sixteenth century and the French during the whole of the eighteenth. In both the sixteenth and the eighteenth centuries domestic events tended to dictate the course of foreign policy: religious issues contributed to anti-Spanish attitudes, and economic ones to anti-French ones. By contrast, in the seventeenth century stumbling foreign policies had repercussions on domestic affairs.

Who were the enemies of England in the seventeenth century? In considering that question one faces the fundamental crisis of the times, for crown and people were often divided upon whom the nation should oppose, and why. James I leant towards the Spanish, but his sympathy brought only antipathy from his subjects. Charles I briefly made war with both France and Spain; his politicians, in some sympathy with a Spanish war but not with a French one, gave him little material help. Charles II favoured the French at a time when their nation was held in distrust. He fought the Dutch twice, once losing public support because the war was ill-conducted and a second time because some felt he had chosen the wrong enemy. The reason for this division of interest between crown and people was partly one of timing; the Stuarts had a knack of selecting the wrong enemy for the given moment. It was also partly due to the nature of the prerogative. In the view of the Stuart kings foreign policy was within their prerogative. Parliamentarians thought otherwise. In this the Stuarts were victims of their generation. In the sixteenth century the royal prerogative in foreign affairs had been scarcely challenged. By the eighteenth century the Revolution settlement had provided a political structure which gave the initiative to ministers. Nor did the Hanoverian monarchs seriously disagree with ministerial policy until the accession of George III.

It is, of course, an easier and more conventional task to criticize Stuart foreign policy than to praise it. Therefore in this book an attempt has been made to find redeeming features where they exist. Stress has been laid on the genuine idealism behind James I's pursuit of the leadership of Protestant Europe and of a Spanish marriage alliance. Both he and his son were concerned with sustaining the interests of their family in the Palatinate while ensuring that Palatinate affairs were not made the occasion for England entering the Thirty Years War despite the importance that Protestants in Europe had attached to the marriage. Indeed, the avoidance of English participation in that war must be to their credit.

It is in Anglo-Dutch relations that the foreign policy of James I and his son is seen at its best, not least because it differed from that which they pursued towards much of the rest of Europe. Emotional ties affected James's attitude towards Spain, France, Denmark and the Palatinate. The crown was personally involved, for matrimonial reasons. Towards these nations James allowed himself to become engaged over a prolonged length of time, in the conduct of policies which the nation as a whole often rejected. By contrast, in his dealings with the Dutch James was more detached. Much happened during his reign between the two countries, but James did not permit it to disturb him deeply. This lack of personal involvement saved him from being out of touch with his subjects. In contrast with Anglo-European policies as a whole, in Anglo-Dutch affairs it is not possible to detect that same division of interest between crown and people. Elizabeth I had called the Dutch 'ancient and familiar neighbours'. In the early seventeenth century both James I and the nation at large were content to see Anglo-Dutch relations in the same light, until events—primarily economic—forced them to think differently. Not until the middle years of James's reign was there any widespread realization that Dutch commercial ascendancy was a serious challenge to English interests. Those who were aware of the fact—and they were a tiny minority, including Sir Walter Raleigh and Sir John Keymer—then expected more of a stand by James against the Dutch than seemed forthcoming. But the difference between that minority group and the crown was one of degree, not of policy.

Charles I's relations with the Dutch were more complex. His reign began with assurances of friendship, but by 1630 it had taken on a Jacobean image—with sympathy towards Spain and mistrust towards the United Provinces. For his last eight years Charles was associated with the Dutch by a marriage alliance. Although this was an acceptable contract to English Protestants, it never made the same appeal to the Dutch, who interpreted it as a dynastic ambition of their Stadtholder, having little value for the Dutch nation at large. In the end Charles was in no position to face the challenge of the United Provinces, but it is fair to say that he recognized the challenge and acted with authority to uphold the interests of shipping and industry.

Yet whatever may be said in defence of both James I and Charles I there remains the ultimate tragedy of 1649. Charles I was not executed because of the foreign policies pursued by himself and his father, but equally those policies had done nothing to placate opposition. Contemporaries gave them no credit for avoiding participation in the Thirty Years War. Indeed, lives that were spared in one encounter were spent in another, and the Civil War was laid at Charles's feet. The voice of the victors was heard in the land. One of those victors was Oliver Cromwell, in whom alone during the seventeenth century is found a sense of purpose concerning foreign policy. Cromwell's major objective was to endorse the role of Protestantism in Europe and establish alliances which challenged the Catholic powers. It was a policy that basically failed, since his potential partners—the United Provinces and Sweden—were less whole-hearted than he was about the cause of militant Protestantism in foreign relations. But Europe in the time of Cromwell was made to know that there was an English standpoint, and the nation was judged accordingly.

That judgement recognized England as a nation with a well-equipped navy, and diplomats of ability in John Thurloe, Bulstrode Whitelocke and William Lockhart. Europeans were far more aware of these aspects than they were of the continuing internal constitutional and political stresses. There was an Elizabethan grandeur about Cromwellian foreign policy—and this parallel also explains some of its outmodedness—which contemporaries recognized and which the Restoration betrayed. Nevertheless it is true that the expense of Cromwellian foreign policy contributed to bringing about the Restoration.

Charles II's foreign policy bore little relation to Cromwell's, though in the early years there was a chance that it might. After the second Anglo-Dutch war he committed England to the Triple Alliance of 1668. It seemed to be a gesture for Protestantism. England was once again thrusting out to lead such continental Protestants as the Dutch and Swedes; the Emperor Leopold I called it a league of heretics. Some Englishmen might have been encouraged by the relaxing of legislation against nonconformists, and by Charles's declaration to parliament that he sought 'a better union and composure in the minds of my Protestant subjects in matters of religion'. They would have been discouraged by the basic militant Anglicanism of Charles's parliament, and by the events, however much then veiled in secrecy, to come in the immediate future. For from this time onwards the Restored Stuarts lived dangerously. Had contemporaries known—rather than guessed at—the terms of Charles II's secret treaty of Dover, his throne might have toppled. His dependence on Louis XIV was secured at the price of English pride. If France's aggressive prosperity had been more generally understood, there would have been a more ready acceptance of the Dutch as friends and neighbours. But, without the benefit of hindsight, French ascendancy and Dutch decline were not easily discerned in the early 1670s. It was to Charles's advantage that his subjects did not know their collective mind on this. Those self-same Dutch, in the person of William of Orange, ironically enough provided the instrument which cost James II his throne.

While no common purpose can be found in their various policies, none of these rulers could ignore the impact of trade on foreign affairs.

The three wars fought against the Dutch were basically economic in origin. In all three England rather than the United Provinces was the aggressor, because she asserted claims to sovereignty on the seas and challenged Dutch assumptions of a monopoly in world markets. The third war had least meaning for the participants—and won the least support in England—because by 1674 both nations were beginning to realize that each of their economies might be allowed to flourish. Their alliance of 1678 confirmed the growing common fear of French political and economic hegemony and crystallized their mutual relationship for the following century.

All three wars won only grudging approval from the head of state, for neither the Stuart kings nor Oliver Cromwell had any real expertize in trade and commerce. Indeed, it is doubtful if any English ruler could lay claim to competence in that field, with the exception of Henry VII. Stuart kings and the Protector were more at home with political and religious issues. They need not be blamed for this deficiency. The merchant classes of the seventeenth century embraced a diversity of interests and talent. There were those who traded through the machinery of companies; those who acted independently; those who were principally buyers; those who manufactured; those who retailed; those who enjoyed monopolies; those who valued doing business with Spain and the Spanish Netherlands; and those who enjoyed privateering. Their economic goals differed. Thus James I's peace with Spain in 1604, made principally on political grounds, met with a mixed reaction among the merchant classes. Englishmen who wanted to trade with Spain were pleased; those who visualized colonial investment or emigration were encouraged. On the other hand, war-profiteers and privateers (greedy in a declining 'industry') were not enthusiastic.

Later James achieved some success in the economic aspect of his relations with the Dutch. He protected the interests of English fishing, and it was unfortunate that his well-intentioned project to manufacture more finished cloth in England, rather than export it to the Dutch for dressing and dyeing, turned sour on him. He recognized fish and cloth as the major challenge of the Dutch so far as European trade was concerned. The full impact of their far eastern interests came in the closing years of his reign and he did little to assert the role of the English East India Company or avenge the insult of the Amboina massacre. At that time there was little he could do.

No direct relationship can be established between Charles I's foreign policy and the interests of trade. His initial four years, 1625–9, brought no benefits and the final nine years, 1640–9, were destructive. Only in the middle years of the reign, 1629–40, were some indirect commercial advantages gained from neutrality abroad and peace at home. English shipping secured a certain amount of carrying trade from war-combatants, and English ports acted as entrepôts for both inter-European and Eastern commerce. As for fish, Charles took a surprisingly strong line against the Dutch at a time (1638–40) of political crises at home.

Whatever goodwill Charles won amongst certain sections of the business community was largely lost by his antagonizing others through giving out corporate monopolies. These were primarily in staple domestic commodities, such as soap and malt, and therefore caused internal discord. They did not affect overall reaction to the crown's foreign policy.

Cromwellian foreign policy saw a return to intervention in Europe and a hazardous imperial enterprise in the West Indies. The former had political and religious overtones; the latter proved economically disastrous. The political status which Cromwell won for England was never matched by economic achievement. Too much money was spent, the Dutch were a continuing commercial threat, fishermen remained unsatisfied, and Cromwell never established good relations with the city merchants, despite his setting-up of a Council of Trade in 1655.

Nevertheless some of the Commonwealth's economic policies survived the Restoration. The Navigation Act of 1651 was re-enacted, the East India Company stayed a permanent joint-stock company, and there was a distinct expansion of trade.

Charles II turned in 1660 from the negative pursuits of an exile trying (ineffectively) to hamper English trade to the positive rôle of a monarch validating the 1660 Navigation Act. This was an assertion of English commercial interests; it was more effective than its predecessor of 1651. Despite evidence of evasion, the Act strengthened the nation's shipping, encouraged further economic growth and endorsed the mercantilist nexus of mother-country and colonies.

Indeed, it is part of the irony of Charles II's reign that he himself was impecunious while many of his subjects prospered. This was partly due to the Navigation policy and partly due to the decision, taken in 1663, to allow free export of money. Once capital ceased to be tightly contained within the realm (as earlier mercantilists had argued it should), it could be bought and sold as if it were a commodity. The logic of this led to the foundation of the Bank of England in the reign of William III.

That Charles II was not unaware of the importance of these trends is shown in his letters to his sister, Madame, but the argument that he allowed his foreign policy to be governed by commercial factors cannot be sustained.

Alone of the rulers who shaped seventeenth-century foreign policy, James II had had experience as a businessman and speculator. He had been a governor of the Royal Africa Company and of the Hudson Bay Company, and was closely associated with the administration of New York after its capture in the second Dutch War. But his brief reign allowed him little opportunity to put this experience to practical use in the interests of the nation's economy.

No seventeenth-century ruler was self-sufficient in his direction of foreign policy, however much it might—in the case of kings— be a matter of royal prerogative. Those closest to the sovereign in decision-making were the secretaries of state, whose influence varied considerably. Abilities, court-favour and parliamentary or diplomatic experience were contributory factors. There were those such as Robert Cecil, Earl of Salisbury, whose background and talents brought them to prominence. There were quiet, efficient men such as Sir George Calvert and Viscount Conway, and men of especial loyalty to the crown such as Sir John Coke and Dudley Carleton, Viscount Dorchester. All these were servants of the first two Stuarts. Later in the century, Charles II's secretaries included such much-travelled diplomats as Sir Leoline Jenkins and Sir Joseph Williamson, both more esteemed abroad than by the House of Commons. James II was ill-served by the Earl of Sunderland.

Accountable to the secretaries were overseas representatives such as Sir George Dowding and Sir William Temple, who might wield influence at Paris or the Hague, or serve in some obscure European outpost forgotten, unsung and unpaid.[1] There were occasional 'prestige' appointments such as that of Bulstrode Whitelocke, sent to Sweden by Cromwell in 1653.

The profession of diplomacy was taught by the French during the seventeenth century. Principles laid down by Richelieu and Louis XIV were eventually embodied in Callières's great volume *De la manière de négocier*. This was not published till 1716 and so no seventeenth-century English diplomat could have benefited from its precepts. But Callières himself was a working French diplomat during the time of Charles II, James II and William III. Perhaps his opposite numbers noticed him putting this precept into practice: 'A diplomatist should remember that open dealing is the basis of confidence. The secret of negotiation is to harmonize the real interests of the parties concerned.' These were counsels of perfection

---

[1] Payment was usually overdue.

and moderation. Unfortunately diplomats had to contend with the back-stage intrigues of kings and the mercantilist economics of politicians.

Seventeenth-century diplomats would meet each other during the treaty negotiations which were a prominent feature of international relations from Westphalia onwards. Indeed the Westphalian settlements, between 1643 and 1648, established a new basis of European co-operation and discussion. The diminution of papal influence, the rise of nation-states and the horrors of the Thirty Years War all made such co-operation necessary. English diplomats were present at such meetings as Aix-la-Chapelle in 1668 and Nymegen in 1678.[1]

Such conferences reminded representatives not only of the importance of their own national needs but also of those of Europe as a whole. Diplomats were led to consider what was best for the stablity of European relations, and strove for equilibrium in the continent. This 'balance of power' was attained by alliances and alignments. In the context of the seventeenth century the pursuit of this doctrine was clumsy and artificial. It bore little relation to economic rivalries and was largely ineffective. Yet this was scarcely the fault of the diplomats. They were (and are) the servants of the rulers and politicians who committed nations to war. On that reckoning English diplomats did not fare badly at the hands of their masters.

During the eighty-five years from 1603 to 1688, England was formally at war for less than a dozen. If one adds on seven years for the civil war, the total is still under twenty. In Europe as a whole there was a war somewhere during seventy-eight of the eighty-five years. The mention of war leads us to consider English foreign policy in relation to defence. Both Europe's armies and navies increased substantially in size. By the end of the century Louis XIV's army accounted for 1 per cent of the French population. By contrast, an approximation for England would be 0·3 per cent, except for the brief period of James II's standing army when the military strength of the nation doubled. No English ruler attempted to have a large

---

[1] The actual date of the treaty associated with Nymegen. Diplomats talked for three years (1676–9).

army. There were several reasons for this, which gained force as the century wore on. Armies were expensive. Recruitment was difficult. Service as mercenary troops was better paid, and accounted for the Englishmen and Scotsmen serving in France, Sweden and the Netherlands. There was a revulsion against militarism after the civil war and the rule of the major-generals during the Protectorate.

If England lagged behind most of Europe in the growth of her army, the same could not be said for the navy. Here she shared in the general increase in naval power and technique common to the seventeenth century. Alone of the Stuarts, James I had no enthusiasm for the navy. He cut back on public expenditure when he could, and only showed interest towards the end of his life when the Marquis of Buckingham took him to Dartford in 1619. Charles I, after the ill-fated naval expeditions with which his reign began, raised 'ship-money' for the navy, asserted the sovereignty of the seas, calling a ship by that very title, and gamely protected English fishing interests.

The navy under Cromwell defied the Dutch, challenged their carrying trade, and made advances in the tactics of combat. The Cromwellian soldier-turned-sailor, Robert Blake, established a reputation comparable to that of the Elizabethan sailors and not matched again till Nelson's day. To the royalist historian and politician, Clarendon, Blake first 'drew a copy of naval courage, and bold and resolute achievement'.

The navy brought back Charles II in 1660 and it always retained his warm support. He constantly pleaded with parliament for money to maintain it, despite the half-million pounds it cost annually. By the end of his reign there were slightly more ships in commission than at his accession. They were largely new vessels of larger tonnage than hitherto. Charles's brother, as Duke of York held office as Lord High Admiral from 1660 to 1673 and commanded the fleet in the second Anglo-Dutch War. Both Charles and James benefited from the administrative efficiency of Samuel Pepys at the navy office, whose achievements, recorded in his *Memoirs relating to the state of the Royal Navy*, cast an eternal sunbeam on the times. Unfortunately Pepys fell from favour in 1679 and did not return to serious work till 1684. In those five years the English navy suffered a sufficient decline to make the nation of little account in European affairs. Such was its importance.

During those years the English navy was less effectively administered than that of France, and suffered by contrast. Louis XIV spent twice as much as Charles II on his navy—he could afford to—and there was an air of efficiency and technical competence in French dockyards which Englishmen, unless spurred on by Pepys, never quite emulated. At the end of the day for James II his navy, which he himself had served so loyally, failed to prevent the landing of William of Orange.

Finally one may reflect upon the moral standing of those rulers who created English foreign policy in the seventeenth century. In this, despite the variation in their policies, there is certain common ground between the first two Stuarts and Cromwell. None pursued a policy for personal gain. At their best James I, Charles I and Oliver Cromwell had the good of the nation at heart. James believed it might be achieved through his idealism, Charles (after 1629) through isolation and appeasement, and Cromwell through restoration of prestige abroad. All three were patriots, and in each was an honesty of endeavour according to his lights. However, the patriotism of Charless II and James II is less explicit, and their severest critics have denied it to them. Both men set themselves goals somewhat different from patriotism. Charles II's pursuit of financial independence was the device which made feasible his concept of absolute monarchy. He believed this essential in the government of nations and therefore fundamental to the governing of England. James II's belief in religious toleration has a certain credibility. Without it, as he said himself, a nation could not be great and flourishing. His foreign policy is largely distinguished by its absence. One is more aware of the effects of his domestic policy upon other powers, especially the Dutch. English reaction to that policy led some politicians to see the colours of patriotism nailed to the mast of William of Orange rather than to that of their own king. It allowed them to justify the Revolution.

Patriotism in the seventeenth century was not the commanding moral stricture which it later became. Religious persuasion and philosophies of government were equally important to those who formulated seventeenth-century foreign policy. Only if we judge the James's, the Charles's and Oliver by the moral attitudes of their own day can we understand the policies they shaped. They were men of their time, seeing their world in a way very different from our own.

2 Uncertain peace, 1603-18

> 'I have ever, I praise God, kept peace and amity with all, which hath been so far tied to my person, as at my coming here you are witness I found the State embarked in a great and tedious war, and only by my arrival here, and by the peace in my person, is now amity kept where war was before'
>
> *James VI and I*

THE PEACE OF 1604

James VI and I inherited both a throne and a war. The former he had coveted for a generation, and rejoiced in its acquisition; the latter he lost no time in abandoning. Within days of his accession on 24 March 1603, English courtiers had arrived at Edinburgh. Amongst many other matters of business, they sought to find out his intentions towards Spain. During the triumphal progress south, in April, there was time to ponder upon the problems of the future.

On reaching London James was greeted by the French minister, Sully, sent by Henry IV. Sully, hoping for support in a general demonstration of strength and unity against the Habsburgs, outlined his master's plans for the future of Europe.[1] But James was non-committal, and Sully departed empty-handed. Another ambassador, the envoy from Venice—noted for his shrewdness—commented on James's ability in negotiations: 'He is capable of dissimulating his feelings, and is averse from war.' It was a view confirmed in the autumn when James gave audience to a Spanish envoy, with whom

---

[1] Sully, in his *Memoirs*, gives a long and fanciful account of these plans, which he calls 'Le Grand Designe'. Not unkindly, they may be seen as the thoughts of a retired statesman with plenty of leisure letting his imagination run away with him.

he agreed that all grounds for hostility between England and Spain had disappeared with the death of Elizabeth I.

It was a convenient solution, if a highly personal one. James himself had no quarrel with Spain. Elizabeth's confrontation with Philip II was related to her own claims to reign. The leading protagonists of the Anglo-Spanish war were dead: Philip as well as Elizabeth, Burghley, Drake, Hawkins, and Medina Sidonia. Furthermore, a peace had been made between France and Spain at the treaty of Vervins in 1598. But, as later events showed, the situation was not as simple as this. Anglo-Spanish relations still held implications for trade, colonialism and religion.

Of immediate concern to James was the expense of the war. Somewhat illogically he indicated it was no concern of a King of Scotland—though he had been vacillating in his attitude to the Spanish Armada fifteen years earlier. He saw Spain as no longer a threat to Ireland and he resented the cost of continued help to the Dutch. Hence English troops serving in the Netherlands were in future to be paid for by the States-General of the United Provinces, and be regarded as a mercenary force.

During the summer of 1604 negotiations towards a peace settlement took place. James asserted English ascendancy from the start by insisting these be held in London. The basic issue between the two countries was the establishment of peace. By August this had been done, and the treaty then signed in London was ratified in Madrid the following May. From the English point of view, an essential adjunct to the negotiations was the future position of trade with Spain. England won the right to trade in Spain and the Spanish Netherlands, together with an assurance that her traders would not suffer for their Protestantism in Spanish ports. Colonial trade was another matter. The English held the view that Spain could only claim exclusive trading rights in those areas of the Indies she had effectively occupied. James accepted this, and rejected Spanish assumption of monopoly over the Indies as a whole. Whatever validity Spain might have claimed for such assumptions in the past—based on agreements such as the treaty of Tordesillas (1494) and the papal bull *Inter Caetera* (1493)—had depended mainly on naval might. With the defeat of Spain at sea, political claims to the monopoly of the New World meant less. Nevertheless, James I had to be content with his own thoughts and utterances on this matter. No clause in the treaty specifically conceded trading rights or settlement claims. Not till the treaty of Madrid in 1670 did Spain recognize the territorial acquisitions of other nations in the New World. By then, England—and other European countries—had effectively colonized lands in both the Americas and the West Indies. James I, from 1604 onwards, pointed the way through the Virginian enterprises.

Thus the treaty of London gave England the confidence—if not the licence—to prospect abroad. Emigrants and investors saw the possibilities of empire, whether dispatching families off to a new life or floating companies for joint-stock enterprises. By the treaty, England withdrew from the European contest against Spain—as France had done in 1598. Spanish-Dutch hostility continued, providing in 1609 an area of diplomacy in which James I could venture.

Despite these advantages, the immediate reaction to the peace in England was unfavourable. War-profiteers saw a loss of income. Militants felt that a few more months of war would have led to the utter defeat of Spain—an argument with little foundation. Protestants resented bargaining with a Catholic power. Nor was the immediate aftermath of the treaty any more encouraging. The Dutch regarded themselves as betrayed. Their own conflict with Spain continued. We shall consider their relationship with England in the first half of the seventeenth century in chapter 5. In European waters, English ships were attacked by Spanish ones if they were suspected of aiding Dutch interests or trading with infidels such as the Turks. Incidents of merchants arrested on the high seas, to face confiscation of goods and charges in Spanish courts, aroused the anger of parliament. James's minister, Robert Cecil, Earl of Salisbury, found it necessary to remind the Commons that relations between England and Spain were a subject for the royal prerogative and not for politicians.

Indeed, the constitutional role of the monarch in foreign policy was understood in 1603, although there had been political inroads into that prerogative during the reign of Elizabeth. James made no specific reference to foreign affairs in his speech at the opening of parliament in March 1604, nor did 'parliament itself do so in the

'Apology' of a few weeks later. But both king and parliament, by their mention of religion, were touching upon a matter related to the nation's foreign policy. 'Let your majesty be pleased to receive public information from your Commons in parliament as to the civil estate and government' contained more than a hint of parliamentary assertion. Six years later such courtesies were ignored: 'Do not meddle with the main points of government: that is my craft' was countered by 'an ancient, general and undoubted right of parliament to debate freely all matters which do properly concern the subject'. That was in 1610. Relations between the two parties went from bad to worse. But up to 1618 it was not in the realm of foreign policy that the major clash of interest lay. The crown's financial weaknesses had made James vulnerable. Revenue devices such as Impositions which allowed him to do without parliament might stand muster in time of peace. They could be no sort of security to James in the event of war. Therefore, it was when James became more fully committed on the European scene, after 1618, that foreign policy became an important aspect of the constitutional and political struggle between him and parliament.

James I was an idealist in foreign policy. He saw himself as a peace-maker. It was a cry he echoed as late as 1619, when there appeared *The Peace-Maker, or Great Brittaines Blessing*, a tract to which he contributed. To his first parliament James spoke of peace, and of the 'great and tedious war' which he had inherited. The fundamentals of his peace philosophy are straightforward: he visualized becoming the leader of European Protestantism who could yet establish a rapport with the great Catholic power of Spain. In personal terms, this seemed to have possibilities. He was the son of Mary, Queen of Scots, but the successor of Elizabeth. He had made overtures to the Catholic interest while King of Scotland, yet had warned its adherents in 1604 not to 'presume upon lenity'. It was a dual role which English politicians found difficult to comprehend and of which Spanish ones were suspicious, even contemptuous. Nor did it recognize the tremendous divisions in early seventeenth-century Europe. The forces of Catholicism and Protestantism, the thrones of Philip III and Henry IV, and the economic aspirations of the Dutch were all detrimental to European harmony. To James's idealist hopes for peace may be added some more practical reasons. The crown at his accession was impoverished, not having shared in the overall expansion of wealth towards the end of the sixteenth century. Not only was war expensive, it also forced the crown to have greater resource to parliament—and thus invited parliamentary criticism. He regarded the issues upon which England had fought Spain as outmoded by 1603 and irrelevant to a king from Scotland. Finally, James was temperamentally opposed to violence.

THE PALATINATE

Much of James's policy in the early years of his reign concerned the affairs of the Holy Roman Empire. In 1609 the dukedoms of Julich, Cleves and Berg became vacant. The region was important in Imperial politics for both geographical and religious reasons. It lay in the lower Rhine valley and had been ruled by John William, a Catholic. Two Protestant princes laid claims, while the Emperor Rudolph II sent troops to occupy the Duchies. To offset the Imperial threat German Protestantism secured help from the French, Dutch and English. James I seconded four thousand troops already serving in the Netherlands. He did not seek war over the issue. But the self-styled leader of Protestantism could not stand totally apart, especially after the assassination of Henry IV in 1610. In the end, his troops did help in staving off Imperial influence, though a settlement, involving division, was not reached till 1614. It was a gesture towards that area of James's foreign policy which was to assume greater importance as he became embroiled in the affairs of the Palatinate.

It was the marriage prospects of James's daughter, Elizabeth, which first led to his involvement with the Palatinate, whose ruler was styled Elector. This meant that he participated actively in choosing the Holy Roman Emperor: a role he shared with six other princes of the Empire. Despite the fact that the elected emperor in the seventeenth century was always the head of the Austrian branch of the Habsburgs—which therefore made an election virtually automatic—the office of elector gave political and constitutional importance to the holders. The Electoral Palatinate had further strengthened its independent position in 1563 when Frederick IV established Calvinism. In 1608 this religious commitment led the Palatinate to enter the Protestant Union. This was an association of German Protestant princes bound together in a military alliance to defend Protestantism in the Empire. Part of its importance lay in bringing Calvinists and Lutherans into some degree of unity. A year later the three ecclesiastical electors—the archbishops of Mainz, Trier and Cologne—together with Maximilian, Duke of Bavaria, took the lead in forming the Catholic League (1609). Both organizations, technically illegal, looked to outside support—the Protestants to France, the Catholics to Spain. It was towards one of these groups of divided militants, the Protestant Union, that James I had already turned when he gave cautious assistance in the Julich–Cleves dispute. He now became more positively associated with German Protestanism in negotiating the marriage of Elizabeth to the Elector Frederick in 1613.

The marriage was important in that it represented a favourable move by James towards Protestantism. European opinion at the time recognized this possibility. A remarkable number of accounts—and of drawings—exist of the young couple, and Calvinists welcomed an English[1] addition to their ranks and an alliance which might help to weaken Habsburg hegemony.

The bride, Elizabeth, was sixteen, the same age as her husband. The wedding in England, in February 1613, was the occasion for expensive and prolonged festivity, the entertainment including a presentation of Shakespeare's *The Tempest*. It is a commentary on the state of James's finances that he did not pay the bill for this production until three months later. Indeed, the expenses for the wedding as a whole, amounting to £100,000, put a millstone round the Stuarts' necks, and was the origin of later financial distress. For the next five years Elizabeth enjoyed a happiness which the political storms of the Thirty Years War were later to deny her. She has her place in English history as the mother of Prince Rupert of the Rhine, and of Sophia, electress of Hanover, herself the mother of George I. James never again saw the daughter who sailed away from

---

[1] In fact, Elizabeth was half-Scottish and half-Danish.

England in 1613. Her marriage had closely identified him with Protestantism, while the political adventures of her husband, five years later, were to bring James I perilously close to becoming a combatant in the European conflict.

ANGLO-SPANISH RELATIONS

Meanwhile, another side of James's foreign policy concerned his relations with Spain, with whom he sought friendship. Contemporary opinion in both England and Spain recognized a change of attitude on the part of princes, if not the people. James had lavishly entertained the Spanish delegates to the peace conferences. Nor was this all. The expedition to Spain in April 1605 to ratify the treaty had been an expensive undertaking, necessary for both diplomatic and prestige reasons. It was led by the Lord High Admiral, the Earl of Nottingham, with a retinue of five hundred. During his six-weeks' stay in Spain Nottingham's dignity and charm 'much graced him with this people'. He reported to James I that the peace was so welcome to the Spanish that they prayed for James as if he were 'their own King'. During his stay Nottingham had been approached by the Duke of Lerma with the suggestion of a marriage between Prince Henry and Anne, the elder of the two daughters of Philip III. Nottingham's authority did not extend to conducting such discussions and he confined himself to stating that the prince would remain a Protestant in the event of a marriage. This proved the stumbling-block to a marriage alliance in repeated negotiations, in 1605, 1607 and 1611. In 1611 the younger Spanish Infanta, Maria, was offered as the candidate in place of her sister, who had been betrothed to Louis XIII following a rapprochement between France and Spain. James was annoyed at the switch of emphasis and looked in other directions. 'There is no one who dare say a word about the second Infanta,' said a courtier. A Tuscany marriage foundered on similar religious rock. Early in 1612 marriage proposals from both Savoy and France were being considered. For Savoy there was a chance of an ally against Spanish masters; for France, a concession to her Protestant subjects; for James, a bridal dowry and a wife for the future king. Sadly, it was Henry who had the last word, in two senses. 'My part, which is to be in love with any of them, is not yet at hand,' he declared. Soon afterwards, in November 1612, after some weeks of ill-health, he died.

The year 1612 marked the end of an era in James's conduct of foreign policy and more particularly in his relations with Spain. Henry's death had been preceded earlier in the year by that of Salisbury, his only minister with ability. James had lost his elder son and his senior adviser. His younger son, Charles, became a candidate for marriage, but James did not choose to find a replacement for Salisbury. ' The king makes no haste to nominate any, but says he is pretty skilled in the craft himself', wrote a contemporary. For two years James had no principal secretary, though he was not without advice. There rose to fame a young Scotsman from Roxburghshire, Robert Carr, whom James had first seen as a page on his journey to England in 1603. James, 'with unsparing hand, loaded with treasures this in significant and useless pageant'.

By 1612 there had emerged in England both pro- and anti-Spanish factions. The 'Spanish' party was led by the pro-Catholic seventy-two years old Henry Howard, Earl of Northampton, who had previously shown sustained sympathy for Mary Queen of Scots. Howard attracted others of his family, including Nottingham, who had led the peace delegation of 1605. The opposing faction contained strong anti-Spanish elements in the lord chancellor, Lord Ellesmere; the archbishop of Canterbury, George Abbot, and the Earl of Southampton. James was not hostile to the existence of such groups. They counter-balanced each other, strengthened his own position and allowed him to pursue his equivocal role towards both Spain and the Protestant powers.

The favourite Carr, although approached by Northampton, had no reason to attach himself to either group, until he fell in love with a Howard. Frances Howard had been married to the Earl of Essex in 1606. In 1613 James appointed a commission which granted her an annulment. By Christmas she had married Carr, who had been created Earl of Somerset. James financed the marriage despite the hardships which led him to call parliament in April 1614.

Somerset, married to a Howard, encouraged James's Spanish interests. The Spanish ambassador in England, Diego Sarmiento,

Count Gondomar, noted his influence: 'the king resolves all business with him alone, both those that pass in Council, and many others of which he never made Council aware'. It was a short-lived liaison. Somerset presumed too much on being the king's favourite. By the late summer of 1614 Somerset would argue with the king, who reproached himself for 'raising a man so high' so that he presumed 'to pierce my ears with such speeches'. Furthermore, James had met Somerset's successor, George Villiers. But the real eclipse came when Somerset and his wife were charged with the murder of Sir Thomas Overbury. Overbury had been reputedly poisoned in the Tower of London in 1613. He had been a friend of Robert Carr's, but bitterly opposed both the marriage to Frances Howard and the Spanish faction surrounding the king. And he knew more than was comfortable about the nullity suit.

The king parted with Somerset in October 1615. The Earl and his wife were tried and found guilty on slender evidence in May 1616, though their death sentences were commuted by James to imprisonment, and subsequently they were pardoned.

Somerset's influence had been brief. While he was in favour (1612–15), James had pursued his pro-Spanish policy, and Gondomar had recognized the advantages of using Somerset as a vehicle for Spanish interests. Somerset's fall had significance for James's foreign policy in that it lowered the king's value in Spanish eyes. He had shown himself unwise in his choice of men, and he had weakened domestic respect for the monarchy.

Meanwhile, the breach between king and his English politicians had widened. Henceforth, James needed Spain more than Spain needed James. His need for Spain was highlighted by his failure to secure financial help from the parliament he had summoned in 1614. The Commons sought redress of grievances, particularly voicing their opinions upon impositions. James in vain sought supply. It was a bitter two months with harsh words said on either side: Sir Edwin Sandys declared that 'This liberty of imposing would break down the foundation of all our interests and maketh us bondmen'. James's reaction to such a parliament was equally sharp: 'I am surprised that my ancestors should ever have permitted such an institution to come into existence. I am a stranger, and found it here when I arrived, so that I am obliged to put up with what I cannot get rid of.'

But he got rid of it, nevertheless, by dissolution in June 1614. In his financial distress, he turned to other revenue devices, such as benevolences; in his political troubles, he turned to other counsels. For the first time—but not the last—a Stuart king sought foreign guidance. Gondomar was at hand. It was he to whom James spoke the words quoted above. Gondomar must have recognized their naïvety, but he capitalized on the situation. James was bereft of help from the Commons and deprived (by death) of the support of Northampton. A Spanish marriage and a Spanish dowry seemed essential for economic survival and personal prestige.

During 1615 and 1616 discussions on a marriage between Charles and the younger Infanta Maria took place. James made all the going. It suited the Spanish to procrastinate, raising such issues as the religious upbringing of children and the worshipping facilities for a Catholic Infanta resident in England. James dared not commit himself to concessions towards English Catholics as a whole, nor could Philip III obtain papal approval for a marriage.

So matters stood until 1617 when Sir John Digby, who had visited Spain in 1611, went back there. The terms with which he was met were blunt: the repeal of the English penal laws; the appearance in Spain of the prospective bridegroom; the establishment of a Catholic church-building in London. Digby's return to England in the summer of 1618 coincided with the return from further afield of another knight and courtier, Sir Walter Raleigh. Both men were the bearers of bad tidings, and their missions were not unconnected. For Digby, the future held the earldom of Bristol and diplomatic activities; for Raleigh, disgrace and the scaffold.

Sir Walter Raleigh had languished in the Tower of London, modestly housed with his wife, son and library, since 1603. A charge of high treason lay against him for conspiring to deprive James of the throne. The evidence had been dubious. Raleigh was a man against whom James had been set before he left Scotland.

James liberated him in March 1616 in order to sail, once more, to the Orinoco river in Guiana. There Raleigh claimed he would find gold deposits without infringement upon Spanish interests. If Raleigh fought the Spanish, his life would be forfeit.

James cannot have been unaware of a Spanish township, San Thomé, on the Orinoco river guarding the mines. Was he sending Raleigh to a deliberate death—either at the hands of Spanish forces or those of an English executioner? It seems unlikely. Undoubtedly mineral wealth was the attraction: possibly Raleigh might secure access to it without a fight. Yet his presence in the Orinoco river valley came dangerously close to a challenge. Unoccupied tracts of Guiana were one thing—James's unilateral attitude to exploration in 1604 gave him claims to forage there. Spanish settlements in the Orinoco valley were another—exclusive rights to colonial territory were being violated.

The clue to James's policy lines in the simultaneous mission of Digby to Spain. A show of strength by the English in the Caribbean might be the device which secured the Spanish marriage. James was not to know, at that stage, the terms with which his diplomat would be presented.

Raleigh sailed in 1617 for the Caribbean with a small fleet and his own son. In the event, his troops landed and—contrary to his orders—attacked San Thomé in a night skirmish. Greek tragedy killed the boy.

Raleigh's arrest in June 1618 on his return to England was inevitable, and only disputed by his friends. His subsequent condemnation was more controversial. Gondomar reported that James would do 'whatever we like to remedy and redress the damage and insult to Spain'. Indeed, Gondomar demanded that Raleigh be handed over to Madrid for execution. James's councillors voiced resentment at this dictation from Spain, only to receive the curt reply that the king would make his own decisions 'without the advice of fools and badly disposed persons'. Philip III indicated he would accept execution in England.

Gondomar completed his first period of duty (1613–18) well satisfied, returning to Spain in July. He had won a major victory for Spanish interests. Raleigh went to the block three months later, to be executed on the charges laid against him in 1603. Only a few commissioners, whom James appointed, were allowed to hear his defence. Raleigh in facing death showed that same dignity with which so many sixteenth-century Englishmen had died.

Raleigh and his kind had shared a jingoistic hostility to Spain which suited their generation. It was a simple nationalism, allied to the cause of Protestantism and tinged with economic ambitions. As the sixteenth century drew to a close these assumptions lost some of their naïvety. By the reign of James I they were caught up in a more complex age. Raleigh, in outliving Hawkins and Drake, faced these new diplomatic complexities and became their first victim.

The departure of Gondomar, the death of Raleigh and the empty suit pursued by Digby made 1618 a profitless year for James. His Spanish policy had brought mistrust. The years of uncertain peace had been without reward. He was about to hover on the edge of the great European war now starting from small beginnings in Bohemia.

3   Intervention in Europe, 1618–29

'If he went to Spain for a wife, he might have had one
nearer hand, and saved himself a great deal of the labour'

Henrietta Maria

FERDINAND AND FREDERICK

Assassinations, whether successful or abortive, underline bitterness
and encourage conflict. On 22 May 1618, the attempted assassination
in Prague of two agents of the Archduke Ferdinand, by throwing
them out of a window, provoked the Thirty Years War. On 28
June 1914, the assassination in Sarajevo of the Archduke Franz
Ferdinand, by shooting him in his car, provoked the First World
War.

The earlier incident—known to history as the Defenestration of
Prague—had arisen over the election of the Archduke Ferdinand to
the Bohemian monarchy. Ferdinand, as was his near-namesake in
1914, was the heir to the Habsburg monarchy and a kinsman of the
emperor of the day. Both archdukes—in 1618 and in 1914—became
focal points of national, slavonic reaction against Habsburg influence
and the authority of Vienna. Both occasions brought Europe to war
on a grand scale. There we must part company with comparisons.
There was no place in the conflicts that led to the First World War
for the great divisive factor in seventeenth-century Europe. For the
basis of that division within Europe was religion. Ever since the
Augsburg settlement of 1555, Catholics and Protestants had pilloried
each other in pamphlets and propaganda. Protestants, although
divided themselves between Calvinists and Lutherans, had seen in
religion a means of weakening the influence of the Emperor. Even
Catholic princes such as Maximilian of Bavaria were not indifferent
to this. Thus religious and political rivalries were to merge into one.
By 1609, as we saw in chapter 2, there were both Protestant and

C

Catholic alignments, while incidents such as the Cleves–Julich succession had been potential opportunities for war. Nor had concessions to Bohemian Luterans, made in the Letter of Majesty (1609) issued by the Emperor Rudolph II, placated Protestants as a whole. Rudolph and his successor, Mathias, had not offered a militant Catholic leadership. This was to come from Mathias's own successor, the Archduke Ferdinand. Ferdinand was a devoted Catholic, educated at a Jesuit university and bitterly hostile to Protestants. The childless Emperor Mathias was urged to nominate him as his successor in 1617. As the Bohemian throne was elective there was an opportunity for the Bohemian nobility (largely Protestant) to put forward a rival candidate. The opportunity was missed through poor leadership and internal dissensions, Ferdinand being chosen without formal opposition as king-elect on 17 July 1617. Two days later, at Mathias's instigation, Ferdinand was crowned king of Bohemia. In the centenary year of Luther's Wittenberg theses, this event aroused bitterness among the Bohemian Protestant nobility. In the following March an imperial decree forbade Protestant meetings. This was a violation of the promises contained in the Letter of Majesty. The decision led the Bohemian nobility under Count Thurn to that confrontation of May 1618 in the Hradschin Palace at Prague with Catholic representatives of the Emperor. Assassination had not been premeditated, but mob-fury led to the men being flung into the courtyard from a height of seventy feet, in the fracas which followed a heated debate. They survived because they landed in a manure heap.

Bohemian opposition to Ferdinand further stiffened when he was elected Emperor on 26 August 1619, six months after the death of Mathias. Two days earlier, rejecting Ferdinand, the diet had elected Frederick, the Elector Palatine, as their king. In one week Ferdinand had lost a kingdom and gained an empire.

Frederick's election to the Bohemian throne was popular in England, where the pro-Spanish faction was declining in influence, partly due to the absence on sick leave of Gondomar; but the event placed James in a dilemma, posing 'the greatest question of his life'. The claims of Protestantism and kinship argued support for Frederick. But there was a powerful case for the other side. James still hoped to bring about a Spanish marriage. Furthermore, he could hardly approve the rebellion of the Bohemians against the claims of legitimate succession. Thirdly, he did not wish to be committed to a war, nor to the summoning of parliament to finance it.

An embassy from Frederick, led by Count Dohna, came in the late summer of 1619 seeking James's approval and support. James vacillated, taking refuge in delay. He considered the legal aspects of Frederick's election and after consulting his councillors rejected their opinions. A contemporary noted that his 'timidity increases day by day as old age carries him into apprehensions'.

Finally, James condemned the Bohemian revolt. Nevertheless he let Dohna depart with the conviction that if Frederick formally accepted the Bohemian crown, James 'would soon declare himself and give his approval'. This was more than the truth but enough to bring Frederick round to acceptance. He showed his defiance of the emperor by marching with 150 coaches and a thousand troops to the Bohemian frontier. His wife, Elizabeth, noted the welcome as 'a great show of love of all sorts of people'. In England there was rejoicing. Even the possibility of his becoming emperor could not be ignored.

The 'winter king' reigned for exactly a year—from his coronation in Prague in November 1619 till his defeat at the Battle of the White Mountain in November 1620. Gradually his enemies crowded in on him and his friends became indifferent. By February Spain had agreed to help Ferdinand by invading the Palatinate. By the summer social division had caused peasants to attack castles, and civilians to refuse bread to starving troops. By the autumn Maximilian of Bavaria's forces under Count Tilly were closing in on Bohemia.

Throughout 1620 James's attitude remained obscure. Gondomar's return to England in March 1620 led the king to reassert his hopes for a Spanish marriage, 'I desire no alliance but that of Spain'. Gondomar indicated Spanish interest in the Palatinate, territorially the entry to the Netherlands. James shrank from an aggressive reply, even declaring (in relation to the Bohemian throne) that his son-in-law was a usurper to whom he would give no help. Gondomar reasonably reported to Philip III that there was little to fear from England. A few months later the Spanish and Austrian sides of the

Habsburgs set about ending Frederick's cause. Spanish troops entered the Palatinate, and Imperial ones Bohemia.

James sent 2500 troops as a show of strength, but forbade them to fight. In this commitment he found some sort of compromise. It was right to defend the Palatinate—Frederick's legitimate inheritance—but wrong to defend Bohemia. Again, it was an example of a personal view whose logic was unacceptable to his people. By November 1620, Frederick was defeated at the Battle of the White Mountain near Prague. James's troops had, of course, not been there and their absence was a subject of latter criticism in England. James—rabbit-hunting at Newmarket—returned to London to face a hostile council urging war. He replied that he could not support the Bohemian cause, but would defend the Palatinate. For James it remained important to localize the conflict. By defending the Palatinate he was safeguarding his Protestant family interests without jeoparding his hopes of a Spanish marriage. Parliament was reluctantly summoned, for the first time in seven years, in January 1621. James, in a long speech, emphasized his desire for peace, but recognized the need for war to defend the Palatinate. Parliament gave a modest grant, then turned to other business—principally charges of bribery against the lord chancellor, Francis Bacon. Meanwhile, Frederick continued to believe that his cause was not lost. James gave him financial help but little positive assistance; 'his irresolution gives me a very great pain', said a French observer. James I can have been in no doubt about the attitude of his Commons. In May 1621 they sought to punish a Catholic lawyer, Edward Floyd, for slighting the Elector Palatine and his family. The Commons had exceeded their powers, but the Lords took up the issue and, acting as a judicial body, punished Floyd ferociously for 'rejoicing at the losses happened to the King's daughter and her children' and 'speaking basely of them'. By the end of the year James and parliament had become deeply divided. A Commons' Petition on 3 December 1621 urged James 'to pursue and more publicly avow the aiding of those of our religion in foreign parts', and hoped that the bent of the war and the point of his sword would be directed against Spain. The extent to which the Commons also attacked Catholicism within England indicated how much foreign and domestic policy were merging into one central issue at this point. James (who had had an advance copy) replied on the same day. He attacked the right of parliament to debate matters 'tending to our prerogative royal'. He attacked the members for arguing and debating 'matters far above their reach and capacity' and rebuked them for presuming 'to meddle with our dearest son's match with the daughter of Spain'.

Far from being submissive, the Commons petitioned again on 9 December 1621. They showed a firm understanding of current events, a fear of Catholic successes in Europe and a hostility to encroachments on their ancient right to freedom of speech. James communicated twice more, denying the right of free speech, and defining it as 'derived from grace and permission'. The upshot of this controversy on Privilege was the Commons' Protestation of 18 December 1621. It was a document which James formally annulled, but he could not reject the attitudes it formulated. Parliament no longer accepted the doctrine of 'forbidden areas', upon which they might not speak. Foreign affairs had come too close for comfort for the security of church and state. It was on a bitter note that James ended the business of the year 1621.

For his son-in-law Frederick, circumstances were no better. Frederick was ready to renounce Bohemia if only he might keep the Palatinate. In the end even this was denied to him. The Lower Palatinate became Spanish, the electoral title passing to Maximilian of Bavaria. Bohemia became a Habsburg territory and remained so until the formation of Czechoslovakia, almost exactly three hundred years later. Possibly James's current favourite, George Villiers, by now Marquis of Buckingham, had given the most sensible advice during the year: 'So long as you waver between the Spaniards and your subjects, to make advantage of both, you are sure to do with neither'. In later years power and pride made Buckingham less objective in his judgments.

SPANISH AND FRENCH MARRIAGE POLICIES

In January 1622 James, having committed certain members to the Tower of London, dissolved parliament, encouraged to do so by Gondomar. Gondomar then resumed discussions on the Spanish marriage, and it became the main concern of English foreign policy

during 1622 and 1623. Gondomar himself was more enthusiastic,
if less realistic, about the marriage than were his masters in Spain.
To the king of Spain the marriage of the younger Infanta to the
heir to the English throne had dynastic value in relation to France.
It also would be the means of securing liberty for English Catholics.
For James the attraction lay in the fulfilment of his ideal—peace in
Europe. It had remained a motive pursued with utter sincerity for
twenty years.

But there were reservations. The alliance could not be brought
about while Spanish troops lay in the Palatinate: 'I like not to marry
my son with a portion of my daughter's tears.'

During 1622 marriage articles were exchanged, but the concessions which they demanded of English Protestantism were more
than James could hope to implement. Early in 1623 Charles decided
to play both diplomat and suitor. Accompanied by Buckingham—
and calling themselves Jack and Tom Smith—they travelled incog-
nito across France to Spain. Charles's unexpected arrival was
outwardly welcomed. He was treated with immense respect in
Madrid, being 'introduced into the palace with the same pomp and
ceremony that attended the kings of Spain on their coronation, while
the Spanish Council received public orders to obey him as the king
himself'. All this was very gratifying, but it fell short of access to
the Infanta Maria, whom Charles might only see in the presence of
the court. Even the words she addressed to him had been set down
for her beforehand, in order that she should say nothing relating to
Charles's suit.

Charles's presence in Spain certainly forced events. James feared
his son might be made a hostage, and this influenced him in accepting
in July 1623, the religious terms of the proposed marriage treaty.
These included alleviation of the penal laws against English Catholics,
though James interpreted toleration to mean private worship only.
But whether Catholic worship was to be public or private, it would
involve a proclamation annulling a statute. 'You now take unto
yourself liberty to throw down the laws of the land at your pleasure,'
declared the archbishop of York. But James rejoiced that 'all the
devils in Hell and all the Puritans in England could not stop the
match'. Yet the match never took place. Two months later Charles

left Spain, and his arrival in London in October was hailed as a triumph for Protestantism. 'True mirth and gladness was in every face', business was at a standstill, bonfires blazed and the choir of St. Paul's echoed the psalmist the delivery of 'the house in noting of Jacob from amongst the strange people'.

Why did a major object of James's policy crumble before him? There are several explanations: Charles, the romantic adventurer, came to love the lady less. Furthermore, he realized that Spain was not prepared to withdraw from the Palatinate. Once it was understood that Charles himself would never be won to Catholicism, Spanish interest became lukewarm. Lastly, Buckingham himself turned against the project. By Christmas another marriage project was in the ascendant. Buckingham, often snubbed in Spain, now dispatched an emissary to France. This emissary, Lord Kensington, reported that the French would not 'strain us to any unreasonableness in conditions for our Catholics', and that they were anxious for an English alliance against Spain.

French policy had so far favoured the German Catholics, and Louis XIII had refused to consider helping the Elector Palatine. But the accession to power of Richelieu in August 1624 brought about a complete reversal of French policy, for Richelieu's aim was to free France from Habsburg pressure on her land frontiers. He sounded England about the chances of an Anglo-French marriage alliance. Buckingham, who had been personally unacceptable to the Spanish during his stay there, was ready enough to break with Spain and persuaded James to summon parliament in February 1624, which promptly sought abandonment of both the Spanish marriage and the cause of the Palatinate. By April James had finally rejected any possibilities of the marriage, largely through the influence of Buckingham, now hailed as the man who had 'dissolved and broken the Spanish marriage'. For the moment Buckingham basked in popularity.

Negotiations for a Spanish marriage in these last years of James's reign were more prominent than those pursued towards France. Yet as early as 1615 Princess Christina of France had been considered as a possible bride for Charles. Four years later the Marquis of Traisnel was sent as an ambassador extraordinary 'charged with

speaking of the marriage of the Prince to Madame Henriette', who
was aged nine and Christina's younger sister. He was given an
entertainment lasting eight hours, with an interval for 'sweetmeats
and wine and ale in bottles', but no French marriage contract
followed. With the defeat of Frederick at the Battle of the White
Mountain, the case for a Spanish marriage and Spanish help became
urgent.

From then until April 1624, as we have seen, the Spanish marriage
was pursued. We have Henrietta's own wry comment on events—
Charles actually saw her in Paris on his way to Madrid in 1623:
'If he went to Spain for a wife, he might have had one nearer hand,
and saved himself a great deal of the labour.'

To the end of his life, James strove hard to cling to the Palatinate,
'I desire not to brook a furrow of land in England, Scotland or
Ireland without restitution of the Palatinate; and in this mind I will
live and die'. It was a vain pursuit. Parliament was not prepared to
finance a war for the recovery of the Palatinate, despite its enthusiasm
of a few years earlier. Just as later parliamentarians rejected a concern
for the monarch's Hanoverian 'business', so did these men think the
business of the Palatinate 'not fit for the consideration of the House'.
If James's recovery of the Palatine were to be effective, aid must
come from elsewhere.

Parliament was ready enough to go to war, but on a wider front
and with national objectives. James was granted three subsidies and
three fifteenths, 'the greatest aid which was ever granted in parliament to be levied in so short a time' (but less than he asked for).
It was given to him to defend the realm, secure Ireland, aid the
Dutch and equip the navy. Parliament's last word to their king a
few days later reminded him that defending the realm meant
enforcing the laws against Catholics. The equation offers the final
explanation of James's failure. His pipe-dream of a Spanish marriage
alliance, with the treaty-terms it involved, was never acceptable to
his subjects. During the last twelve months of James's life—March
1624 to March 1625—English foreign policy changed in character.
Policy-making was dominated by Charles and Buckingham, with
the ageing James in a subordinate role. Their personal objectives
were to recover the Palatinate without any Spanish bargains, and to

associate themselves in general with the enemies of the Habsburgs. The change of policy led to renewed approaches to France, and initial approaches to the Netherlands and the Scandinavian countries. The French marriage therefore became imperative. By December 1624 negotiations had reached the treaty stage. Again a Catholic power demanded concessions relating to the upbringing of children in the Faith and to the indemnification of Catholics as a whole. James, who had promised parliament 'no such condition' would be 'foisted in any other treaty', was persuaded by Buckingham to accept the terms. The new French minister, Richelieu, anxious as he was to secure English support, had interests of his own. France's concern was to avoid Spanish encirclement. A vital feature of Richelieu's policy was to secure control of the Valtelline pass between Italy and Austria, a strategic valley then in Spanish hands. It was Richelieu's prior concern with this territory, and with the wider implications of Habsburg Italian interests, that made him indifferent to the Mansfeld expedition. Count Mansfeld, a soldier of fortune who had found employment in the Thirty Years War, was appointed by Buckingham to command a joint Anglo-French expeditionary force designed to land on the continent and attack the Habsburg interests. Richelieu's success in the Valtelline in November 1624 made the force unnecessary for specifically French purposes, nor would Richelieu have them land and needlessly antagonize the Spanish. When James died Mansfeld's troops were still unemployed, and dying in their thousands from disease.

Despite these distractions, the French marriage came about. On 1 February 1625, the *Mercurius Britannicus* carried an advertisement for a booklet on Charles and Henrietta Maria, which might be bought together 'with a lively picture of the prince and the lady cut in bronze'. James's death delayed the ceremony, but it was conducted by proxy in May 1625, and Henrietta Maria arrived in England the next month.

England's second gesture in these twelve months was towards the Dutch, with whom a treaty was made in June 1624, offering six thousand English troops to help in the ultimate attainment of independence. Finally, envoys made approaches in the Baltic. Swedish terms, as proposed by Gustavus Adolphus, were more expensive than James could afford. Danish proposals, made by Christian IV, were more reasonable. In February 1625 the two kings agreed that England would pay for seven thousand men in return for a Danish campaign in Germany. The idealist path of a Spanish marriage and the leadership of Protestant Europe which James had followed was abandoned by the entry of Charles and Buckingham into the more mundane ranks of the anti-Habsburg forces. His policies seemed now to be converging with the religio-political feud which the Thirty Years War had become. It was not what he would have wished.

James was an old king at the right time. In the early years of his reign his hopes for a peaceful European scene were not purely romantic; exhaustion after the late sixteenth-century wars gave peace a chance. By 1625 the vista had faded, and Europe was sternly at war. Understandably, James played little part in the events of the last few months of his life. The French ambassador recorded that 'sickness renders him incapable of deciding anything'. He was euphoric and melancholy by turn, and physically in bad condition. By March he was dead. He had never deliberately provoked his parliament on constitutional issues, but both he and it had anticipated the great controversies of the next reign. He had sought love desperately, yet died with little real affection felt towards his person. He had always lived as a man of peace, 'that great peacemaker, Britain's peaceful king', yet in death bequeathed to his successor an obligation to fight in Europe in enterprises expensive, precarious, and not always relevant to English interests.

WAR AGAINST SPAIN AND FRACE

The new reign's first act of aggression against Spain was in October, when a fleet of eighty vessels and fifteen thousand soldiers and sailors under Sir Edward Cecil, nephew of James's minister, Salisbury, sailed for Cadiz. Their failure to achieve success was due to a variety of reasons which included bad leadership, lack of supplies, and disease. Expeditions like those led by Mansfeld and Cecil largely comprised untrained men, usually conscripts, the best of whom however had remained at home for national defence. War with Spain continued intermittently, but Charles's efforts were hindered by lack of money and public support. Even more damaging to his personal position was the outbreak of war against France in 1627. Despite the marriage of Charles to Henrietta Maria shortly after his accession, several factors brought England and France to war.

In the closing months of James's reign, while an anti-Habsburg alliance was still possible, English ships had been lent to help the French against rebellious Huguenots at La Rochelle. The refusal of the crews to fight against fellow-Protestants weakened relations, especially when French shipping was taken for prize in the English channel, as ransom for the ships loaned to Louis XIII. Meanwhile Buckingham had already angered both Louis XIII and Richelieu by his attempts to charm the French Queen when he had gone to France to bring back Henrietta Maria. The snub he received made him determined on 'a war with that kingdom'. Consequently, during 1626 Buckingham was responsible for various attempts to irritate the French. Some of Henrietta Maria's attendants were dismissed and, more seriously, attacks on French commerce continued. Not surprisingly the French retaliated against English shipping. The French were also aggrieved when they realized that there was to be no relaxation of the penal laws towards Catholics.

By 1627 Buckingham's influence brought the two countries into direct confrontation. La Rochelle still remained a Huguenot stronghold, held by the Duke of Soubise. Soubise visited England and secured the promise of English help. Buckingham himself led the expedition which attacked the French fortress at the Île de Ré. He was beaten, not only by the counter-attacks of the enemy, but by the indifference of the Huguenots themselves, who were not aware of his arrival. Not content 'with dishonour and slaughter', Buckingham attempted a follow-up in 1628, which Richelieu repulsed with barricades across the channel leading to La Rochelle. By his failure Buckingham joined Mansfeld and Cecil in having led an expedition doomed to fail through disaster and disorganization. All these did nothing to improve the military record of the first two Stuarts.

Thus, neither in his campaigns nor his commitments did Buckingham achieve anything. While he was busy fighting the French and the Spanish he was forgetting recently-agreed obligations to the Danes and Dutch. In December 1625 the treaty of the

Hague confirmed the alliances with Denmark and the United Provinces. The treaty was all part of the plan for a coalition against the Habsburgs. It achieved nothing. Hopes of bringing France into the coalition were dashed when Buckingham's policies led him into war with France. Furthermore France and Spain made peace with each other in 1626. Nor could men and money be forthcoming to help England's new allies in the Thirty Years War. The Danes, in particular, were badly let down by the non-fulfilment of English promises. Christian IV was beaten at Lutter in 1626. He wrote to England deploring the lack of aid, and was forced to sue for peace at Lubeck in 1629, retaining only his hereditary lands against the Imperial forces of Ferdinand fighting in northern Germany.

Shortly after the Île de Ré fiasco Buckingham was assassinated at Portsmouth by a disgruntled army officer, John Felton.[1] Apart from personal animosities, Felton saw Buckingham as the 'cause of every national grievance, and as the great enemy of the public'. Buckingham's death attracted few mourners—'the obscure catastrophe of that great man', said a contemporary newsprint. Between Charles's accession and Buckingham's death relations between king and parliament had deteriorated. In Charles's first parliament Sir Nathaniel Rich urged him to use the advice of councillors when making war. Others criticized the idea of concessions to Catholics in the French marriage treaty. His second parliament met in 1626 in the shadow of Cadiz and with the prospect of a conflict with France. The one had been a disgrace and the other would be an expense. Sir John Eliot made the attack on the government a personal one on Buckingham when he declared that the loss of honour, men and ships was due to 'those we trust' and not the enemy. This was the signal to impeach Buckingham in a massive document of almost ten thousand words, the work of eight men over three weeks. The basis of their charge was that Buckingham had abused his power, made personal profit and delivered ships to the French to serve against the Huguenots. Buckingham presented a twelve thousand word reply to the House of Lords on 8 June 1626 and Charles dissolved his second parliament a week later.

[1] Felton served at sea although he was an army officer. Naval lists had not yet begun.

Buckingham's impeachment showed how much he was disliked and distrusted by parliament. In his own person he had widened the gap between the crown and the politicians. He countered effectively many of the charges made against him relating to neglect of duty, pluralities, sale of office, and giving medicine to James I which hastened the king's death. Yet the impeachment did not mention the issue that really mattered—Spain.

Why had Buckingham committed England to war with Spain? There seemed to be a general assumption that the Spanish had been insincere all along in their negotiations over the marriage. In the prevailing anti-Catholic climate this was an acceptable view. Buckingham did not stand indicted for leading England into war with a country against whom there was a strong tradition of hostility. Yet there were aspects of the negotiations in Madrid which never reached the ears of the Commons. They never knew that Buckingham had become convinced that the Spanish marriage would work to his own disadvantage, and that Spanish influence on the king of England would supersede his own. He had told the Spanish minister, Olivares, to expect from him 'all possible enmity and opposition'.

The man who knew most was the English ambassador in Spain, the Earl of Bristol. On Bristol's return to England, Buckingham poisoned Charles against him and tried to forbid him a writ to attend the House of Lords. But Bristol's personal accusation of high treason against Buckingham said far more of significance than the Commons' impeachment. Bristol made it clear that Buckingham had been personally antipathetic to the Spanish. However, Bristol's opinions were unimportant to a parliament pledged to dislike Spain. And because they disliked Spain, they should have given Charles more financial help in the war against Spain. In a sense Parliament condoned the war, yet hindered its conduct because of religious and financial grievances.

In the interval between Charles's second and third parliaments came the Five Knights' Case and the outbreak of the French War. The incidents were connected in that the five men (in the end, only four) had refused to pay a forced loan which Charles had required of them to finance the war. 'Not a penny of those monies which thus we borrow of them shall be bestowed' except on war expenditure, he had promised. The courts upheld the crown's right both to impose the loan and imprison the defaulters. It became the main principle at issue in the third parliament, taking precedence over Buckingham's affairs, and it led to the Petition of Right (1628). This was a declaratory statement on the nature of the law, and was concerned to secure the law's benefits for subjects, and to assault the growing range of discretionary prerogative powers assumed by the crown. Charles accepted it, so that his subjects might 'have no cause for complaint', but neither he nor the crown lawyers saw it as detracting in any way from his prerogative.

Parliament followed up the Petition by a Remonstrance against Tonnage and Poundage. Although there was careful recognition of the historical precedents for this source of crown revenue, the Commons felt that Charles's political behaviour put restraints upon his entitlement. Their attitude was enough to cause him to prorogue parliament on 26 June 1628. It was on 23 August that Felton struck down Buckingham.

The business of the second session of Charles's third parliament was mainly financial and religious culminating in the protestation (March 1629) against innovations in religion and the levying or payment of tonnage and poundage without consent of parliament. Charles ended the session of a few weeks on 10 March 1629 and dissolved the parliament. For eleven years parliamentarians met in the wilderness, or John Pym's lodgings.

Buckingham's death had ended the brief period of simultaneous conflict with France and Spain. The war had always been of the duke's making rather than the king's. Nor could Charles finance it further. Within a month of the dissolution of parliament peace with France was made in the treaty of Susa (1629). Negotiations with Spain took longer, agreement finally being reached in the treaty of Madrid (1630). These were the policies of the crown—not of parliament. The king and his minister had launched the wars; now the monarch, sole survivor of the partnership, ended them.

Since the policies had both been mistrusted and unsuccessful, Charles I had alienated parliament and a large section of the merchant class. Yet the fault was not entirely his. His parliament at its last meeting had been mainly concerned with religion and finance, while individual MPs had remarked on the defeat of Protestantism in Germany and France and the power of the Imperial forces. Charles saw this too, and there was much to justify his final comment to them: 'our affairs were put into a far worse case than at the first, our foreign actions being disgraced and ruined for want of help'. Buckingham might have bungled less if parliament had paid him more.

4   Europe and the English Civil War, 1603–49

'It hath been observed that a French queen never brought any
happiness to England. Some kind of fatality, too, the English
imagined to be in the name of Marie, which it is said the king
rather chose to have her called by than the other, Henrietta'
Lucy Hutchinson

A PERSONAL FOREIGN POLICY

In 1641 Charles's opponents took him to task in the Grand
Remonstrance, both for 'the precipitate breach with France' and for
'the peace with Spain without consent of parliament'. They had
therefore welcomed the peace with France made at Susa in 1629,
but had distrusted the treaty with Spain made at Madrid a year later.

But there were convincing reasons why Charles should retain the
pacific state of affairs he had established in 1630. He thus avoided
the expense of war—and its concomitant, the summoning of
parliament. It was arguable that European issues did not affect
England, and that as the Thirty Years War pursued its course
neutrality with security was the best posture to adopt. Yet by this
avoidance of the war Charles was held by some to be lowering
English prestige. Where were Englishmen to be found participating
in 'The Protestant Cause'? And even if they could be found, as at
the siege of Breda in 1637, why were they without official support
from the king's government? This was the tone of those who were
ready to use any stick at hand to beat the king with. It took no
account of the fact that England, by her participation in the European
conflict, was unlikely to alter its course. Certainly, by 1632 'The
Protestant Cause' seemed safe and the war became more concerned
with the secular interests of the participating powers. Conversely,
the major nations of Europe saw the military power of the English

king more at risk, and hence of little use to them in their own designs.

This is to take a broad view of events. Closer examination reveals that while Charles avoided war, he had considerable contact with the combatants, some of whom were ready to court his favour during the 1630s. In this chapter, therefore, we shall examine two main aspects of the period 1630–49: the foreign policy of Charles I in the 1630s together with European attitudes towards him, and secondly, the relations between Europe and England during the Civil War.

At the basis of Charles's foreign policy in the 1630s lay the perennial issue of the Palatinate: the woof in the web of all his endeavours. The king hoped that both France and Spain might help him in restoring the exiled Frederick to his electorate, and he also had expectations from Sweden. His genuineness impressed his sister Elizabeth, the Elector's wife: 'I am so confident of my dear brother's love and the promise he hath made not to forsake our cause', she wrote. Indeed, when the 'cause' of the Palatinate and the 'cause' of Protestantism coincided, Charles's policies were found acceptable by his subjects. The Grand Remonstrance, for example, spoke of the desertion of the Palatinate. It was when the Palatinate seemed less immediately involved that Charles's identification with Protestanism for its own sake seemed suspect. In 1631 Protestantism's champion was Gustavus Adolphus. He had been the victor against the Imperial forces at Breitenfeld and had little need of English help. Moreover, so long as the English king was still associated with Spain, he suspected his motives in offering help. English and Scottish troops, paid for by Charles and led by the Marquis of Hamilton, fought with Gustavus, primarily with the object of recovering the Palatinate, while Frederick himself joined the Swedish king's retinue. But Gustavus felt he could conquer Germany on his own without their aid, nor was he prepared to restore Frederick except under certain conditions.

The situation changed the following year, when both Gustavus and Frederick died within the same month. Gustavus fell at Lutzen (October 1632) and Frederick died of a fever while visiting his Palatinate which Protestant forces had overrun in 1631. Their deaths had an impact upon Charles's policies. Sweden's new regent, Axel Oxenstierna, was more favourably disposed to the English king than Gustavus Adolphus had been—welcoming both his money and his commitment to the Palatinate. Charles for his part felt even more strongly attached to the interests of his nephew, Charles Louis, the new elector. But in giving Oxenstierna far less money than was needed for a successful campaign on the Upper Rhine, Charles was letting slip the chance for positive action on the new elector's behalf. Yet what else could he do? He had little money to spare and could obtain no more without summoning parliament. And if parliament did meet, there was no guarantee that it would grant him sufficient finance to pursue an active policy in Europe.

However, two years later, in 1636, Charles might have been able to establish for himself an important alliance in Europe, and finally see his nephew restored to the Palatinate. The background to this was the peace of Prague (1635), involving the emperor, Ferdinand II, Saxony and Bavaria. By it Maximilian of Bavaria retained his hold on the Palatinate and only financial and personal-property concessions were made to the late elector's family. This led Charles to send John Taylor as his envoy to Vienna to see if he could reverse the Prague decision. Taylor, a diplomat of limited experience, was able to report in March 1636 that the emperor was prepared to remove the Imperial ban on Charles Louis, receive him and 'enfeoff him with no mean proportion of his father's inheritance'. Upon this 'confident assurancy of Taylor' Charles decided to send to Vienna the Earl Marshal of England, the Earl of Arundel and Surrey. By contrast with Taylor, Arundel was an experienced diplomat and also a politician who had crossed swords with Buckingham, mediated in the Petition of Right debates and was later to preside over the trial of Thomas Wentworth, Earl of Strafford. During the journey to Vienna one of his staff wrote an account of the condition of Europe after nearly twenty years of war, where people were 'found dead with grass in their mouths' and towns and villages were 'battered, pillaged or burnt'. Arundel himself was horrified at what he saw. In this respect Charles I did his country no disservice when he kept her out of the European holocaust. But a commitment to war on the Imperial side was just what Arundel found was expected of him. There was a distinction between a *foedus arctissimum*—a restricted and severe agreement with specific terms—between England and the Empire and a *foedus tam offensivum quam defensivum*—an agreement as much offensive as defensive. Arundel was reluctant to commit England to wholesale war against the emperor's enemies, the Dutch and the French, even for the sake of the Palatinate. Negotiations finally broke down after Maximilian of Bavaria had pointed out to the emperor that England's support was not worth having, since Charles could hardly finance his fleet and was on bad terms with his politicians. Neither Spain nor Bavaria wished to see the restitution of Charles Louis to the Palatinate. To the Empire 'the old confidence and tried friendship of Spain and Electoral Bavaria' was more valuable than 'an untrustworthy alliance with England'. Arundel's mission was over and he returned to England conscious of having been snubbed. Yet rejection of the Palatinate claim had always been predictable. If to Charles it was the focal point of his foreign interests, to both Austrian and Spanish Habsburgs it was a peripheral matter. To the Austrian branch of the family Catholic interests in Germany were more important. To the Spanish branch the Palatinate was only important as a possible means of securing English maritime aid; whether such aid was of consequence to Spain depended on the immediate strength or otherwise of the French and the Dutch. In 1636, when Spain's forces were doing well in the Netherlands, English help was unimportant. But in 1640, for instance, English aid was much more worth having, and Spanish ambassadors tendered for it.

Despite the failure of the Arundel mission Charles was still hopeful that something might be done for Charles Louis, asking Wentworth in June 1637 if he should 'join with France and the rest of my neighbours to demand of the House of Austria my nephew's restitution, and so hazard (upon refusal) a declaration of war'. This came near to making the Palatinate the occasion for joining the European war, but it proved a decision from which Charles shrank. The ultimate restoration of the (Lower) Palatinate to the Elector Charles Louis in 1648 owed nothing to the Stuart kings, who had for so long attached such importance to it. The Palatinate had involved Charles I in contact with the European nations as a whole, and we may now turn to examine specifically relations between him and Spain from 1630 to the Civil War.

Throughout the 1630s there were two main aspects to Anglo-Spanish relations: the abstract prospect of an alliance and the concrete exchange of mutual material aid. One example of the former was a scheme for an Anglo-Spanish invasion of the Netherlands, first mooted in 1631, and laid aside 'for a fit consideration after'. Charles was concerned over the threat of Dutch power—which he seemed to recognize more clearly than did his subjects—and Philip IV was alarmed at the dual threat of both Dutch and French. Though the alliance had prospects for both parties, it came to nothing. Mutual material aid may be illustrated by an agreement of 1630 under which Spanish silver was minted in England and sent in English ships to pay Spanish forces in the Netherlands. Such vessels were technically neutral, and Charles got his percentage for ensuring a safe passage for Spanish bullion. By the end of the decade it was not only money but also men whom Charles's ships transported, actions which gave the Dutch reasonable grounds to challenge English vessels in the English Channel and capture over a thousand Spanish troops. These incidents were the prelude to a greater confrontation in October 1639, the Battle of the Downs. Spanish ships in the Channel were burnt and sunk, or surrendered to a Dutch fleet which had lain for some weeks watching them as they sheltered off the Downs, while the English navy, uncommitted by its king, watched the encounter. Charles had tried to play the broker to both sides. For a sum he offered to help the Spanish. In exchange for the restoration of Charles Louis to the electorate by Dutch influence he would stand aside. Eventually battle was joined with no bargains made; it had un-favourable implications for Charles's foreign policy. The Spanish saw how frail was the prospect of an alliance with Charles, while the Dutch measured the strength of their fleet in a victory which, ironically, pleased the king's subjects as much as it dismayed the king himself. More than ever the Battle of the Downs revealed the discord that existed between Charles I and his people, who rejoiced at Spain's crushing defeat as they watched from the coastline. Yet despite this episode Charles had one more chance to come to a firm understanding with Spain. Spanish envoys met Strafford on 5 May

1640 to discuss the regular convoying of their troops to the Netherlands, even holding out the prospects of a marriage between Charles's daughter and the son of the king of Spain, and a very large sum of money, in return for a permanent convoy of warships to guard their troop-carriers.

This would have brought together England and Spain in an alliance much stronger than one intended for purely economic benefit. Yet it failed to materialize, for several reasons. Strafford, Charles's main negotiator, fell ill at a crucial point in the discussions; French and Dutch diplomats worked hard in London to hinder them; influential English politicians led by Pym did all they could to prevent an agreement. By the autumn of 1640 Charles finally abandoned any idea of an alliance with Spain, and the haphazard relationship of the 1630s was at an end.

Charles, besides keeping on reasonably good terms with Spain throughout the 1630s, between 1637 and 1640 also considered allying with France. During those years there took place a series of negotiations between France and England, in which Richelieu, through his representative Bellièvre, was more enthusiastic than Charles I. It was in the French interest to weaken Anglo-Spanish ties and, in particular, to restrict the naval help given by Charles to Spain to support the campaign in the Netherlands. For Charles the main motive for continuing the dialogue was to let the Austrian Habsburgs fear that he might indeed make an alliance with France. As we have seen, he hoped this might be a sufficient threat with which to win back the Palatinate.

But neither Richelieu nor Charles I can really have anticipated an alliance. The suggestion for example that English ships should attack the Spanish Netherlands—and even Spain itself—which was made by the French in February 1638 cannot have had much validity for an English king drawing Spanish money and advised by a minister, in Strafford,[1] who favoured a pro-Spanish policy. Furthermore, the presence in England of Marie de Medici, the exiled French Queen Mother, and a bitter opponent of Richelieu, was a further irritant to the French. By May 1640 France had abandoned

---

[1] At that time (1638) he was still Viscount Wentworth.

the idea and withdrew Bellièvre. Richelieu doubted the value of an alliance with a king so patently weak, while releasing from confinement the young Elector Palatine whom he had been holding as a political hostage. Yet Charles's policy had served its turn. Perhaps it was best not to have made an alliance with France yet worthwhile to have let his Spanish allies know what he was doing.

We may notice, briefly, Charles's relations with the United Provinces, which are discussed more fully in chapter 5. Broadly speaking, he pursued a policy strong in its defence of the English fishing interest, and one which won him less support from his subjects than it might have done. It involved him in an integral part of his domestic policies, which caused him much unpopularity. In order to police the seas against foreign vessels, of which Dutch fishing fleets formed a part, from 1634 onwards Charles embarked upon his policy of raising ship-money.

His claim to ship-money was based upon his need for shipping to defend the kingdom and protect its commerce. Charles's lawyers defended his right to be 'the sole judge' of danger. In a long and detailed argument, Sir Robert Berkeley, a justice of the king's bench, held that the object of ship-money was not to provide a revenue device in itself, but to provide the means for having ships. Since the king was bound 'to defend his people against foreign enemies', he must have 'the arms and strength' with which to do it. The constitutional and political implications of ship-money provided a major cause of discontent between Charles and his subjects. Men felt that their property rights were at stake, and were even less reconciled when they saw the ships for which they had paid being used to further a policy that seemed pro-Spanish and unnecessarily anti-Dutch. But for an island-kingdom a navy is fundamental, and Charles must be credited with a genuine concern for the nation's safety. One ship-money writ spoke of the dangers inherent '*in his guerrinis temporibus*'. The times were indeed warlike, and Charles did well to achieve neutrality with dignity and security. Eventually, Dutch resentment at Charles's naval policy led to that conflict at the Downs in 1639. But two years later, in 1641, Charles's elder daughter, Mary, was to marry the son of Frederick Henry, the Dutch Stadtholder. The marriage took place in the month that

Strafford was executed. As the events of 1641-2 took their course the clouds were darkening over Charles. The Long Parliament had come together to collect 'manifold griefs' to 'fill a mighty and vast circumference'. Strafford fell: as out of place in the England of the 1640s as Raleigh had been in that of the 1600s. By December 1641 the Grand Remonstrance was ready. Here were fifteen thousand words of anguish and antipathy. To Oliver Cromwell, they were so important that he would have quit the land if the Commons had not passed it; to Lord Falkland, they were the raking over of events best cast into oblivion; to the Venetian ambassador, they were sedition discrediting a monarch. Not long after Christmas Charles quit his capital and moved to York. On 22 August 1642, with eight hundred horse and three foot, he raised his standard at Nottingham. Civil War—the bitterest expression of human conflict—had broken out. 'I detest this war without an enemy,' wrote the Roundhead, Sir William Waller, to his Royalist friend, Sir Ralph Hopton.

What was the attitude of Europe to the Civil War? At first it produced no significant reaction—war was no novelty to the busy participants in the thirty-year conflict. The 1640s saw the concluding phase of that struggle, and the long diplomacy that led to the Westphalia settlement in 1648. The impotence of England suited her European neighbours, and we need attach no importance to the service rendered by mercenary troops from the continent in the English Civil War. This was a professional business, and worked both ways. Mercenaries from England and Scotland were also found serving in Europe. Nevertheless for the Dutch and the French at least the war eventually came to mean something more. As we have seen, Charles's daughter had married into the House of Orange in 1641. This gave the Stadtholder an interest in the Royalist Cause and he did all he could to encourage Englishmen in Dutch service to return home and fight for the Royalists. In contrast, his subjects tended to sympathize with the parliamentarians, comparing the English hostility to things papal and Spanish with their own historic struggle. Dutchmen also recognized that Charles I was a more astute critic of the Dutch commercial challenge to England than many another Englishman. But Dutch enthusiasm waned after 1647, and the nation shared in Europe's general horror at Charles's execution.

French interest in English events arose out of the policies of Mazarin. In the year in which England's Civil War broke out he had succeeded Richelieu as the principal agent of French government and diplomacy. His concern that Charles should not be defeated led him to send thirteen[1] different diplomatic officials to the British Isles during the period 1643-9, including two to Ireland, in 1644 and 1647. To Bellièvre he remarked that 'the bad example offered by the Scots and English against their king' might be followed by 'the subjects of other princes'. French diplomatic methods were superior to those of any other nation in the seventeenth century, largely due to the exacting influence of Richelieu. The men whom Mazarin dispatched to the court of Charles I—wherever that court might be— had been fully briefed in their mission. Their instructions required them to discover how they could contribute to saving Charles his throne. At the same time they were realists: if Charles had to lose, they were expected to know with whom a French government should subsequently deal.[2] One such man was Jean de Montereul, who spent most of 1646-8 in England and Scotland meeting Scots Covenanters, King Charles and various parliamentarians. His task was to persuade the Scots Covenanters to stand by Charles, to urge the king to consider acceptance of the Scots National Covenant, and to suggest the revival of the historic 'auld alliance' of France and Scotland, against the English. By December 1646 he had failed. The bitterness of internal divisions and the reluctance of Charles to make such concessions to the Scots as the abandoning of the Anglican episcopate had made failure inevitable. For Charles the days of freedom were over. He went from Scotland to England as the prisoner of his subjects. Montereul's role, on behalf of his master,

---

[1] By comparison, Richelieu employed twenty-one diplomats in England between 1624 and 1643.

[2] Early in the eighteenth century, French ambassadors were told in their instructions that it was not 'regarded as offensive' in England for them to have relations with the opposition. One cannot speak of an opposition in the same constitutional sense in the seventeenth century, but clearly Mazarin made contact with Charles's opponents.

had been political. The object had been to preserve the English monarchy: not only because of the nature of that institution itself, but also because Mazarin believed there was less to fear from an England under Charles than from a Republican England which might threaten France's declining naval strength. For the moment an alliance with England was out of the question. Yet France clearly needed England—'to counterbalance the might of Spain', as Richelieu once declared. 'Close relations' with her were 'important', Mazarin recorded. Accordingly not long after Charles's execution, Mazarin resumed an active diplomacy towards the Republican government. Was Charles foolish to spurn French help? The price of a Franco-Scottish coalition against his English enemies was high, the breaking-up of the structure of government in the Anglican church; it was too high for Charles. Nor, indeed, was it a likely possibility. The alliance had little appeal for Presbyterians in Scotland.

Spain played far less part in the English Civil War, confining herself to an unfulfilled plan for sending troops to Ireland in December 1641, at a time when Charles's own critics were making the most of Irish discontents. Spain had her own domestic problems which effectively forbade her becoming embroiled in English affairs. Since the middle ages there had been a union with Catalonia, while Portugal had come under the Spanish crown in 1580. In 1640 both Catalonia and Portugal revolted, thus bringing Spain itself to a state of civil war, which eventually lost her Portugal and bred increased resentment among the Catalans, who held out until 1652. The Spanish minister, Olivares, in fighting the Catalans, exhibited that same horror of war as Waller had shown in England. 'My heart admits of no consolation that we are entering an action in which, if our army kills, it kills a vassal of his Majesty'. This parallel leads us to consider another aspect of events in England in relation to the wider European scene. Contemporaries saw the English Revolution as a specifically insular event, arising for the most part out of issues unique to English society, such as the standpoint of Anglicanism and the attitudes of the Puritan gentry. It was a view preserved for later generations by the Whig historians. Yet the case for a wider comparison goes beyond the emotional reactions of Waller and Olivares.

The English Civil War was in part an expresson of resentment against absolutist power, and it arose mainly from those who felt the challenge to wealth and property posed by royalist bureaucracy. It was of course much more than that, and we may allow it its 'special' English characteristics. But in the political and economic context the nature of the opposition was similar to that which weakened the Spanish monarchy and brought to an end Olivares's career.

Nor were events in France dissimilar. Richelieu and Mazarin had indeed strengthened the country, but at the expense of setting up a governmental despotism that lasted till the Revolution in 1789. Richelieu's own authority was strong enough to resist the challenge of the nobility and of the plots to overthrow him, even when they commanded the support of the king's mother, Marie de Medici, and the king's brother, Gaston, Duke of Orleans. Mazarin, as a newcomer and a foreigner,[1] had to run the gauntlet of opposition from both the nobles and the business classes. The impulse behind that opposition was both political and economic, in that it sought to widen the basis of power and reduce the burden of taxation. This animosity came to a head in the Frondes, between 1648 and 1653. Such events provided a further reason for Mazarin to avoid a more positive intervention in the English war. However much events in England may be seen as distinct from those in the rest of Europe at the time, there were common forces at work in terms of political resistance and economic claims. But when the English executed their king, contemporary Europeans firmly persuaded themselves of the differences between their own affairs and those of England. To the average European observer this was an attack on the mystique of kingship itself, and 'the most horrible and detestable parricide ever committed by Christians'. But the show must go on. Only a short time after 30 January 1649, the diplomats of Europe were recognizing the legality of the new English government, following the example set by Spain.

We have considered Europe's attitude to the English Civil War; but what view did Englishmen take of Europe? In general, the participants in the Civil War gave very little thought to European

---

[1] He was an Italian who became a naturalized Frenchman in 1639.

affairs. The parliamentarians had more to fear than Charles from European intervention, since they had little doubt as to where the support from such 'establishment' figures as Mazarin, Olivares or Frederick Henry would go. Although spies and unofficial agents of information were dispatched to various European countries, the only one with any diplomatic credibility was René Augier, a man of Huguenot origins, who served in France from 1644 to 1649.

Charles I was more conscious of the possibility of European help. His wife was prepared to go to desperate lengths to secure it. Before the Civil War broke out she had been in touch with Catholic sources of supply and aid. She spent the larger part of 1642 at the court of Frederick Henry, the Dutch Stadtholder, returning to England in February 1643 to face a parliamentary hostility even greater than that offered towards her husband. She finally left England in 1644 to live in France, where she continued to raise money for Charles. She had constantly corresponded with Mazarin but to little effect. Henrietta Maria is one of the many tragic figures of Stuart history. She was the daughter of an assassinated king and an exiled queen. The fate of Henry IV made her particularly concerned for her husband's throne; the experiences of Marie de Medici prepared her for her own years of exile. She parted in 1644 from her husband on the upper reaches of the Thames not far from Abingdon, where in happier days she and Charles had taken barge to Oxford. In poverty and ill-health she spared nothing to save his throne. Ironically, she had done more than most to make it in need of salvation. Charles himself was less of a correspondent than Henrietta Maria. But among his letters there survives a belated appeal in August 1646 to Lord Jermyn, the queen's secretary and commander of her bodyguard, asking him to 'begin to press France, both to declare for my restoration, and set some visible course on foot to order it'. A few months later Charles expressed the hope that the European powers, currently making their own peace settlements, would then have time to help him. Indeed, a letter from Henrietta Maria gave him grounds for support: 'Mazarin has assured me that the general peace will be made before Chrstimas (1646), and when that happens you will be properly aided.' Yet no aid came.

IN DEFENCE OF THE KING

Charles I's handling of foreign policy has received harsh criticism from historians. It has been condemned as inept and inconsistent. Yet it is possible to offer a more sympathetic appraisal. After 1630 there was clearly a change from the recklessness which had brought England into war with both France and Spain. It was the issues of those days which did him most harm, such as the raising of forced loans to finance Buckingham's troops at La Rochelle. Ineptness may have characterized Charles's stubborn line on the question of sovereignty on the seas, but there was also a genuine concern for the fishing business, the status of the navy and the threat of the Dutch. Inconsistency may have been behind the frequent but fruitless negotiations with other powers, but underlying them all was a definite moral determination: to restore the Palatinate to his family and to keep England at peace.

Fundamentally Englishmen distrusted Charles's sort of peace, which had too Spanish—and Catholic—a flavour. This anti-Spanish attitude of mind persisted and led a critic of Charles in 1639 to claim that those who ruled England were 'as much Spanish as Olivares'. As early as 1627 Isaac Pennington had written, 'We may enjoy peace and prosperity. I mean peace with all the world, but war with Spain.' Charles's opponents sought both the promotion of Protestanism, and prosperity in fighting the Spanish. Yet Charles too had his views on the nature of prosperity. It was to be won by a policy of non-intervention. There is also a favourable case to be made for his care for the welfare of the poor, at the expense of the interests of the rich, during the period 1629–40. This may have been in the mind of that extravagant partisan, Edward Hyde, Earl of Clarendon, when he proclaimed, of those years, that 'the kingdom enjoyed the greatest calm and the fullest measure of felicity; to the wonder and envy of aïl parts of Christendom'. Quite apart from the fact that the years of the Civil War detracted from the 'felicity' of peace, we must accept that advocates of appeasement have their critics. To what extent was it important that England, by her loss of power, ceased to be of influence in Europe? Did this contribute, as the nineteenth-century historian J. R. Seeley argued, to the rise of France to the position she held in the reign of Louis XIV? Did it matter that no English voice was heard in the Westphalia negotiations? Did the policies of Charles cause Cromwell to re-think England's role in the world? An appraisal of Charles I's relations with Europe between 1630 and 1649 cannot ignore such questions.

5 Anglo-Dutch rivalry, 1603-49

Holland, not so big as one of your Majesty's shires, hath
belonging to it 20,000 sail of ships, which is more than England,
France, Spain, Portugal, Italy, Scotland, Denmark, Poland,
Sweden and Russia have all put together and they build every
year 1000 new ships

Sir John Keymer

DUTCH ACHIEVEMENTS

In his relations with the Dutch, James I's foreign policy was seen
at its best. He recognized the growing importance of the United
Provinces as a nation. He was broadly in tune with English opinion.
He acted with firmness, as when he told Dutch envoys that they
were like leeches and bloodsuckers, seeking to ruin his realm; with
discretion, as when he reminded them that their interests were 'next
to his own in affection'; and with a concern for English trade when
he declared: 'You hinder my own subjects from fishing in my coasts.
When I raise the question, you will not agree to a single word being
spoken.'

At the start of the seventeenth century, there seemed every chance
of good relations between the English and the Dutch. The two countries had fought for many years against Spain, sharing a common
bond of political-religious identity, which had resulted in some
emigration from Flanders to East Anglia. To such refugees had been
added the more transitory visits of merchants, fishermen, scholars,
divines, politicians and artists. If Englishmen admired Dutch art,
farming and banking, Dutchmen were attracted by Puritan theology
and the political ideas of the House of Commons. But observers
such as Thomas Mun and Lewis Roberts, respectively representative
of the middle-aged and young merchant of the 1620s, soon recognized that most of the advantages lay with the Dutch. The advant-

ages were to become more evident as the century wore on and pointed to an English inferiority, which helps to explain the gathering tension in seventeenth-century Anglo-Dutch relations. It was not long before economic rivalry outweighed the mutual appeal of culture and theology.

When James I came to the throne the United Provinces represented those seven northern states of the Netherlands which had formed a union against the Spanish at Utrecht in 1579. Thanks to the leadership of William the Silent, John van Oldenbarneveldt and William's son, Maurice—supported by geographical advantages, Calvinist determination and economic effort—the Dutch secured a twelve-year truce with Spain in 1609. This gave the Dutch the political assurance with which to underline their economic performance.

Amsterdam became a financial centre and business entrepôt, where Europe's businessmen exchanged information, raised loans and established their credit. The Bank of Amsterdam, founded in 1609, acquired a monetary security which survived the uncertainties of the Thirty Years War and an economic depression in 1637, and which retained a predominant position well into the eighteenth century.

Thrift, hard work and opportunism were the bulwarks of this prosperity, in which industrial and commercial expansion was expressed through shipbuilding, light industry and the search for markets. Timber from Germany and Sweden built the new *fluyt* merchant ships. They could be built economically; their broad beam, three-masted rigging and lateen mizen gave them an ugly appearance, but the Dutch were not concerned with aesthetics. *Fluyts*, if slow, were reliable and capacious. Indeed, the ability to build ships for a particular purpose is part of the reason for the Dutch success. Other ships were built to specifications which suited them for whaling and timber-carrying. English merchants were not above buying Dutch vessels.

Industries grew up, handling such varied commodities as silk, china, woollen goods, linen, optical instruments and books. Of these, the printing of books had an especial importance. Jan Linschoten's *Itinerario*, published in 1595, sold in several languages. An English commentator hoped it would encourage the use of 'wooden

walls'. Indeed, it did. Dutchmen, as well as Englishmen, used the
book as a geographical guide in sailing to the East and to the West.
Men such as Cornelis de Houtman pioneered the exploratory voyages that led to the foundation of the Dutch East India Company.
Others explored the Americas or, nearer home, established trade
relations with Constantinople, Venice, Sweden and Russia, whilst
the visit of a Russian embassy to the Hague in 1614 ensured a virtual
monopoly for the Dutch merchants in Muscovy.

But the 'wooden walls' had another use besides the pursuit of
markets. They established the Dutch fishing industry as a fundamental basis of the nation's economy. 'The herring keeps Dutch
trade going and Dutch trade sets the whole world afloat' wrote a
contemporary. The new techniques in shipbuilding and in the
salting of fish brought Dutch sailors wealth in the waters of the Baltic, the North Sea and the Atlantic, and also led them into conflict
with the English.

This was the nation which James I, as early as 1585 (when he was
only eighteen), had seen as a possible ally in his concept of a Protestant Union in Europe, and the matter was again discussed in 1594.
But Elizabeth, resentful of Scottish interference in European diplomacy, had excluded James from the consultations which led to a
formal Anglo-Dutch alliance in 1598.

JAMES I'S DUTCH POLICY

James at his accession—and for some years afterwards—was
mindful of one aspect of that Elizabethan alliance, for the Dutch
had ceded to England two towns, Flushing and Brille, and the fort of
Rammekens (known collectively as the 'cautionary' towns), as
security for their debts. Their possession made the Dutch 'depen-
dants on his favour' and gave the impoverished king one of his
few redeemable assets—towns for cash. Politically this fact made
him underestimate growing Dutch strength, and led him to make
his peace with Spain in 1604 with scant thought for Dutch interests.
The Venetian ambassador thought James was over-optimistic if he
imagined that the Dutch would also make peace with Spain, 'I do
not know if they would be so ready to yield as the king of England
promises himself'. That commentator also noted the decline of

English naval strength, in contrast to its 'increasing force and vigour among the Dutch'.

When peace came between Spain and the Dutch it was principally on Dutch terms. The United Provinces were recognized as independent for the period of the Twelve Years Truce. James was persuaded by Salisbury to promise the Dutch aid if Spain violated the Truce. It was a promise won reluctantly from the king, who not unreasonably asked why England should be ruined to maintain the Dutch. Salisbury countered by pointing out that an isolated and threatened United Provinces would seek France as an ally. Yet Salisbury was as much aware as James of Dutch maritime power. He noted the two thousand sailing ships which lay off the English coast at any one time. The fishing they were engaged in seemed both to him and to James 'a means of daily wrongs to our own people that exercise the trade of fishing'. So ran the words of the king's Proclamation of May 1609, requiring all foreigners fishing off our shores to have a licence. It cast a net which enmeshed Anglo-Dutch relations for decades. James was overruling a concession which the Dutch had enjoyed since 1295, and which had frequently been renewed by English kings, notably Henry VII. The Proclamation brought protests from Dutchmen who had read the recently expounded doctrine of the freedom of the seas in Hugo Grotius' *Mare Liberum*.[1] James, by now thoroughly aware of the commercial strength of the Dutch, was at one with his people in his concern for the livelihood of English—and Scottish—fishermen. Negotiations in 1610 brought a stay of execution of the proposed fishing tolls. English and Dutch sought to avoid a 'show-down': both had respective neighbouring political crises—the Palatinate and Juch-Cleves—of greater immediate concern. The representatives of the States-General were told: 'As for the matter of fishing, his majesty thinketh not fit to spend any more time on it: in the meantime, things may remain in the same state as now they are.' The subject of fishing-tolls lay dormant for a few years, but was raised again in 1616 and in the last years of James's life.

---

[1] Grotius' book, published two months earlier, dealt with the exclusive claims of Portugal in the East rather than those of England round her shores, but the argument was equally applicable.

E

James was without a chief minister for two years after Salisbury's death in 1612. It was a time when Anglo-Dutch relations had sharply deteriorated, but the king had plenty of advice on hand. The imprisoned Raleigh wrote a pamphlet stating that the Dutch sought 'the whole trade and shipping of Christendom into their own hand' and 'the command and mastery of the seas'; he had been one of the first to be conscious of the challenge of the Dutch, in his *Observations touching trade and commerce with the Hollander*, written as early as 1603. This long pamphlet had made a direct appeal to James on his accession to encourage English trade, by countering 'the policy of merchant strangers, who now go beyond us in all kinds of profitable merchandises' and to increase shipping and manufacturing so that all nations would 'veil the bonnet to England'. By 1613 his renewed pleas had been joined by those of Tobias Gentleman, who deplored the challenge to commerce: 'look on these fellows that we call the plump Hollanders, behold their diligence in fishing, and our own carelessness'. The anonymous 'J.R.' feared the threat to the navy. 'If we want (lack) ships, we are dissolved.'

The challenge was both commercial and military and this connection between commerce and force was well illustrated by another fishing crisis which arose at this time. In 1613 the English had annexed the Spitsbergen islands for whaling. Dutch resentment of this action led James to talk with all the grandeur of a Spanish monopolist: they were 'interlopers in lands belonging to our people'. By 1618 rival fleets had done battle off Greenland. The incident endorsed Raleigh's words. Fishing bred mariners who were ready to try their hands at the techniques of naval gunnery. The navigation acts of a mercantilist age were meaningful: indigenous merchant navies were ready to fight. On the whaling issue James took a strong line, at a time when there was some criticism of the general inertia of his foreign policy: 'the worthy deeds of our forefathers form the topic of conversation', said a contemporary, who noted that men were full of 'loud praises for past times'.

But James was a reluctant man of war. He preferred policies of appeasement when it would have been all too easy in the troublesome times of 1618 to hurl England into the Thirty Years War.

On the eve of that event it is convenient to note two ways in which James's financial affairs were linked to his Dutch policy. Dutch manufacturers had been accustomed to receiving unfinished woollen cloth for dressing and dyeing. This ended in 1614 when James I gave the monopoly of the manufacture and sale of dyed cloth to Sir William Cockayne and his associates. James also withdrew the charter of the Merchant Adventurers, who had hitherto exported the unfinished cloth. The whole project, while acceptable in mercantilist terms, proved disastrous in the realm of practical economics and politics. Cockayne's firm was guilty of bad workmanship; the Dutch refused to import finished cloth and produced their own; James I was forced to restore the *status quo*, by ending Cockayne's monopoly and restoring the Merchant Adventurers' charter. But the damage was done. Good trade was lost, the English textile industry went into depression, and there was unreasonable, if understandable, resentment against the Dutch. The second incident affecting James's finances related to the cautionary towns, which, as we have seen, James held as a security. The Dutch resented this obstacle to their full sovereignty, and in 1616 Oldenbarneveldt—as one of his last acts of statesmanship, before he fell due to the turmoil of Dutch domestic politics—redeemed them for cash. The surrender of the cautionary towns was rightly interpreted in Europe as a sign of growing Dutch strength and English weakness.

Fish and cloth represented a direct European challenge to English commerce. Overseas the business of the Dutch in the East Indies offered a different kind of rivalry to English interests. We must briefly examine what the Dutch achieved in the East, and contrast it against English endeavours.

The Dutch East India Company was established by the States-General in 1602, with a monopoly of trade from the Cape to Magellan's Strait. Its wide powers included the right to establish colonies, mint money and make war or peace. All Dutchmen might become shareholders, and the company soon commanded substantial assets. By 1612, backed by a perpetual monopoly and supported by the government, it was inviting long-term joint stock investment.

In the first half of the seventeenth century company ships conveyed administrators, soldiers and traders to the East Indies. In 1611 Pieter Both, the first governor-general of the East Indies, took up office at Bantam in Java. Thereafter under him, and later Jan Coen, Dutch influence spread throughout the archipelago. With the capture of Malacca in 1641 the Dutch secured strategic control of the East Indies, and established an internal Asiastic trade, while the voyages of Willem Janszoon in 1606 and Abel Tasman in 1642 revealed the coastlines of New Guinea, Australia, Tasmania and New Zealand. But geographical exploration—still less settlements— were of minor importance to the Dutch. The sole objective of all their enterprises was trade—the production of balance sheets which reflected the profits to be made in spices.[1] Treaties with native rulers, whether alliances or protectorates, were only means to an economic end.

But the Dutch were not the first Europeans in the East. They faced two European rivals: the Portuguese and the English. The Portuguese had preceded them by a century—since Vasco da Gama had brought home a cargo of cinnamon and pepper in 1498. By 1612 the Portuguese eastern empire was in decline. One of the many contributory factors to this situation illustrates the contrast between Portuguese and Dutch: Portuguese ships were unreliable, and thirty per cent of those which sailed to the East between 1580 and 1612 were lost. The Dutch shipbuilders would not have tolerated such a wastage. Gradually the Portuguese were ousted from the East In- dies, although they retained a dwindling hold in the sub-continent of India.

It is the rivalry of the English, rather than the Portuguese, which concerns us. The English had established their East India Company in 1600. It differed in several ways from its Dutch counterpart. It lacked government support, being instead a chartered monopoly encouraging private enterprise. Its financial resources were smaller and its investors only temporarily committed. Not till 1657 did it become a permanent joint-stock company. Such comparisons be- tween the two companies are unfavourable to the English. But we should realize that the national role of the East India Company was then of less importance to the English. Its ultimate contribution to the history of India could not be foreseen. For the moment it

---

[1] Spices meant pepper, cloves and nutmeg.

represented a trading incursion by a nation which also farmed extensively. The Company's activities could not be regarded as directly within the orbit of the crown's foreign policy, though James I became concerned when finance or prestige were at stake.[1] Up to 1618 the two companies traded in comparative harmony, although there were instances where the English were forced to resort to smuggling rather than open trade.

The outbreak of the Thirty Years War led to some improvement in Anglo-Dutch relations. Indeed, the last seven years of James I's reign found the king in a much stronger bargaining position than he had been since 1609, highlighted by the presence of Dutch envoys in England for a total of twenty-eight months in the period between December 1618 and James's death in March 1625. They came on four different missions, the longest lasting from December 1621 to February 1623.[2] The fact that it was the Dutch who made the journey on each occasion is indicative of English diplomatic advantage, during a period when the United Provinces were at some political risk on three grounds. Their internal affairs were complicated by the political and religious split between Remonstrants and Contra-Remonstrants; the outbreak of the Thirty Years War was more likely to cause them distress than the English; and their Truce with Spain was drawing to a close.

The first three conferences between the English and the Dutch were concerned with the issues raised by the fish and cloth disputes and with the growing tension in the East. In January 1619 James, encouraged by the Spanish ambassador, Gondomar, threatened war against the Dutch if they continued to fish English and Northern waters, but by the summer tempers on both sides had cooled. The Dutch were allowed to continue to fish, on sufferance, and the matter was set aside for a further three years. James also reached agreement over a division of the spice trade, and for a concerted attack

---

[1] Financial affairs as well as foreign policy governed James's lukewarm relations towards the East India Company in that he gave licences on various occasions to interlopers such as Sir Edward Michaelmore and Sir James Cunningham to trade in the East in defiance of the Company's monopoly.

[2] December 1618 to August 1619; February 1621 to April 1621; December 1621 to February 1623; February 1624 to June 1624.

on the Portuguese in the East Indies. Four years of modest co-operation followed, although a strong connection between decisions
taken in Europe and their implementation in the East cannot be
established.

During 1620 James was closely bound up with the fate of the Elector Palatine and particularly susceptible to Gondomar's influence.
Indeed, the pro-Spanish policies towards which both the ambassador
and Buckingham were leading the king were one reason for the return of Dutch envoys in February 1621—out of sight was out
of mind. James insisted that 'fishery questions concerned his right
and honour', and refused to discuss any prospective political alliance
to offset the imminent expiry of the truce. But he reserved his
strongest attacks for the third delegation, whose fourteen months in
England were totally unproductive. It was these envoys who were
called leeches and bloodsuckers, and who were told 'You have in the
Indies a man who well deserves to be hanged'. That man was Jan
Coen, who had become governor-general of the Dutch East Indies
in 1619 and whose independent activity against the English reached
a climax in February 1623, when some merchants on the island of
Amboina were arrested, tortured and executed. Of this James
was still unaware. Had he been so, the envoys might have been
even more conscious of the prejudice they observed in him 'against
themselves'.

For a year—from February 1623 to February 1624—the Dutch
left James alone. They were momentous months for the foreign
policy of his reign. The heir to the throne went to Madrid in pursuit
of his Infanta, and returned empty-handed. English delight at the
final collapse of the Spanish marriage brought a reversal in policy.
Sir Dudley Carleton, the ambassador at the Hague, in December
1623 assured Maurice of Nassau, the Dutch Stadtholder, that James
had always been affectionate towards the Dutch 'during their late
domestic disputes'. He had shown 'care in settling our East Indies
differences' and 'patience in conniving at all the misdemeanours and
insolences of their seamen'. Maurice may have doubted the truth
of this, but he swallowed his pride and dispatched a fourth embassy in
February 1624. Its arrival coincided with that change of direction in
English foreign policy we discussed in chapter 3. Spain was now the

avowed enemy, and parliament was ready to help the Dutch against her. Despite the news of the Amboina massacre (which reached England in May 1624), a treaty was made with the Dutch in June 1624. Troops were promised, and dispatched within the month, to help in the relief of Breda, besieged by the Spanish.

The Amboina massacre marked the end of English activity in the East Indies. Henceforth English interests were concentrated in the sub-continent of India. James may be exonerated from the charge of not avenging Amboina on four counts. In the first place, his part in foreign affairs during these last months of his life was a subordinate one. Secondly, Coen's conduct was that of a colonial governor far from home and choosing to act independently. It might be compared with the later concept of 'No Peace beyond the Line'. Thirdly, he was at one with contemporary opinion in regarding affairs in the East Indies as secondary to European interests, partly because independent activity was in itself less important than governmen policy. Politicians who were not themselves beneficiaries of the Company's monopoly would have agreed with this, although an economic theory of empire was gradually emerging which argued that all classes of society benefited from trading factories and plantations. Fourthly, beyond a diplomatic protest, what *could* he have done? 1624 was no time to create a furore over Amboina when Charles and Buckingham were looking for Protestant allies, amongst whom the Dutch would be included. Nevertheless the pamphleteers got busy over the massacre, and significantly their remarks were reprinted in 1651 and 1672. Amboina rankled throughout the century.

CHARLES I'S DUTCH POLICY

When James died he left England committed to the Dutch by an alliance that was to be further strengthened by Charles I. On the whole it was a policy out of accord with James's general attitude towards the Dutch. There had been moments when he had loved and esteemed them, as the Venetian ambassador reported, and occasions when he visualized the prospects of an alliance based on their joint sea-power. But the diplomat, Sir Ralph Winwood,[1] gives

---

[1] Windwood died in 1617.

us the truer picture of James's policy: 'he is resolved not to swallow, much less to digest, their indignities'. The similarities between Dutch and English were the snare. Precisely because both were traders and sailors did rivalry emerge. James, so often following a Spanish will o' the wisp, showed more realism in his Dutch policy.

His son had come to the throne committed in various directions in Europe by the events of the preceding twelve months. Since his policy was basically anti-Spanish, it was important for Charles to follow up the treaty made with the Dutch in 1624 by a stronger bond. This was done in September 1625, with the treaty of Southampton, an offensive and defensive alliance which gave the Dutch access to all English possessions. Despite the treaty Anglo-Dutch relations did not prosper, for several reasons.

As part of the treaty terms the Dutch participated in the Cadiz expedition in October, and thus shared in its failure. The seat on the Council of State of the States-General occupied by the English ambassador was, after June 1626, declared to be no longer one of right, but of courtesy. England resented Dutch merchants illicitly trading with the Spanish. The question of fishing-rights was again raised. The principal delegate, Jacob Cats, departed from London with 'the dignity of knighthood' but no assurances. Frederick Henry, who had been Dutch Stadtholder since April 1625, was seen to be pro-French in his sympathies at a time when Anglo-French relations, despite the marriage of Henrietta Maria, were turning sour. Charles I had no wish to lose Dutch friendship and dispatched Carleton to the Hague in May 1627 'to prevent the practices of the French who seek to make a purchase of the affection of that state' and 'to provide that no misunderstanding grow upon such overtures of pacification as are made unto us by the Spaniard'. As an expression of his good intentions Carleton was instructed not to mention fish! Carleton's mission failed to allay mistrust, and a busy period of diplomacy between 1628 and 1630 still left Charles I dubious of Dutch policy towards France, and Frederick Henry dubious of English policy towards Spain. Charles's peace with France at Susa in 1629 was acceptable to the Dutch, but not his peace with Spain at Madrid in 1630. By 1630 Charles I had reverted to the peace policies of his father, assuring the Dutch that his benevolence to

France and Spain also extended towards them. The Dutch had become politically and commercially more powerful than ever. This was underlined by the activities of the West India Company, which had been founded in 1621 and which was to last till 1674. The expiry of the truce left the Dutch free to challenge the Spanish in the West, and the objectives of the new Company were as much war and piracy as trade. The Dutch established themselves in three main areas. In the West Indian islands Curacao became, after 1634, the centre for a salt industry and the strategic base for trading in the Caribbean. In South America Surinam (Guiana) remained the only Dutch mainland possession, after a brief attempt to challenge and control the Portuguese sugar interests on the Brazilian coast. In North America a settlement at New Netherland pioneered later colonization along the Hudson River valley. Although populations were small—there were probably no more than 1500 in New Netherland by the middle of the century—the communities served the important function of establishing a carrying-trade between European and colonial ports. Politically the greatest Dutch achievement was the capture in 1628 by Admiral Piet Heyn of a Spanish treasure-fleet off Cuba. It was the first successful challenge to the Spanish monopoly in colonial waters. It may be said to mark the point after which it should have been important for England to take more heed of the United Provinces than of Spain.

A simple view of events might therefore suggest that it was in Charles I's best interests to pursue a *laissez-faire* policy. He had set aside his parliament in 1629, an action constitutionally valid if politically unwise. He had no advisers of ability to whom to turn.[1] He could ill afford foreign ventures. Nevertheless in the period up to the Civil War Charles proved to be frequently involved in Europe's affairs, as we saw in chapter 4. So far as the Dutch were concerned, he kept a wary eye on their pro-French policy, especially after the two nations made an alliance in February 1635. Charles, in retaliation and in defiance of English coastal interests, agreed to

[1] Sir Dudley Carleton (Viscount Dorchester) had a wealth of diplomatic experience. Although elderly by this time, he was the same age as archbishop Laud who served Charles's religious policy throughout the 1630s and beyond. But Carleton played no real part in public life after 1628, and died in 1632.

assist them with naval help against the Dutch. The Dutch reaction was to send an envoy to England in March 1636 to try to win Charles to the anti-Habsburg cause—partly with the bait of restoring the Palatinate to the king's nephew, Charles Louis.

They met with unexpected rebuffs. Charles, raising again the question of fishing licences, presented them with Selden's dictum on the exclusive sovereignty of the British seas[1] and refused to hold a conference, stating 'there could be no debating about his Majesty's rights already confirmed publicly before all the world'. There was dignity and pathos in the stand Charles took against the Dutch between 1638 and 1640. He clung tenaciously to the doctrine of his exclusive right to the seas, threatened action against Dutch fishermen, and yet hoped a Protestant alliance might pursue the Palatinate cause. But by this time the Dutch had realized that Charles could contribute little to the main issues of the European war. By 1639, under the influence of Richelieu, they were far more concerned with attacking the Spanish than either placating Charles or winning him back his Palatinate interests. This policy led them in October of that year to the destruction of the Spanish fleet in the English Channel at the Battle of the Downs. The Dutch, in infringing English waters, defended themselves by saying it was justified by the treaty of Southampton. But by this time they had little need to make undue apologies to England. All through the 1630s Charles had allowed Spanish bullion for the payment of troops in the Netherlands to be shipped in English ships (technically neutral) by way of London to Antwerp. Yet it was only when the king allowed troops to be shipped in English ships that the Dutch acted. Charles, as we saw in chapter 4, in dallying with the Spanish between 1635 and 1639, had supported the wrong side—tactically, politically and diplomatically. For neither Spain nor the anti-Habsburg nations needed the alliance of England's king at a time when his stock and resources were so low. Charles had attempted to be an opportunist—and an unsuccessful one. Yet his policies were not entirely blameworthy. He had been genuinely concerned over English fishing interests and he had faced the prospect of a hostile Franco-Dutch coastline on the other

[1] John Selden, *Mare Clausum seu Dominium Maris*, 1635. Selden wrote it in 1617, but Louis had not thought it wise to allow it to be published.

side of the English Channel. Before the onset of the Civil War one minor diplomatic success came his way when his eldest daughter Mary married William, the son of Frederick Henry, the Dutch Stadtholder. This apparent volte-face by the king was the result of the worsening domestic situation in England in 1640 and 1641. Desperate for aid, Charles was forced to listen to overtures from the Stadtholder.

Frederick Henry's motives were personal rather than national. He was seeking royal prestige for the aspiring Orange dynasty. His negotiator, Cornelius van Aerssens, presented to Charles the arguments for a formal association with the United Provinces rather than continued dalliance with Spain: 'By this marriage you will gain for yourself a first claim on the affections and interests of his Highness and the United Provinces, while if you seek kinship with a house of greater power than your own, you can expect nothing from their ambitions.' Charles, indeed, had hoped his eldest daughter might marry into the Spanish royal family, despite his own experiences at Madrid. But a Spanish marriage by 1640 held less attraction, and Mary eventually married William in May 1641. They became the parents of King William III of England. The Dutch marriage gave Charles the support of Frederick Henry in the years that followed, but its value was more benevolent than effectual. Frederick Henry himself gave Charles what help he could during the Civil War. He lent him money, connived at the supply of arms, and later gave a home to the royal refugees. Henrietta Maria came over and stayed a year, principally to raise support for her husband. 'She kept asking me so piteously', records a Dutch diplomat, 'if there were not any hope that by any means your Highness could be persuaded to assist her.' Frederick Henry did his best until his death in 1647; but the States-General took a neutral stand, while the Dutch people pointed to comparisons between events in England and their own struggle for liberty. But enthusiasm gave way to horror as the final climax of events in England was reached.

The States-General despatched an embassy to London to plead for Charles's life. Their approach to Cromwell and others on 28 January 1649 came too late. Charles was executed on January 30. In a prepared statement a fortnight later, the Dutch envoys were

thanked for their good intentions and sent away with a vague declaration of goodwill 'for the general good of Christendom as well
as our own'. There was a curious epilogue. The Republicans in
England sent an envoy, Isaac Doreslaer, to the Hague in May to
establish good relations. He was promptly assassinated in his hotel.[1]
It was a macabre ending to the Anglo-Dutch relations of the first
two Stuarts. The Dutch, to whom both James and Charles had
frequently been a source of irritation, yet mourned their passing—
and indeed in due course acclaimed the succession of Charles II.
They had cause to do so, for the English Commonwealth was soon
to show itself a far more dangerous foe to the United Provinces than
the first two Stuarts had ever been.

---

[1] Probably by Scottish royalists, but the affair considerably embarrassed the
States-General.

6 Cromwell: the Dutch and the Swedes, 1649–54

Abroad a king he seems, and something more.
Andrew Marvell

THE DUTCH

'He must have had a wonderful understanding in the natures and humours of men, and as great a dexterity in applying them, who from a private and obscure birth without interest of estate, alliance or friendships, could raise himself to such a height.' So wrote Clarendon of Cromwell—by the nature of things, his enemy. He was generous towards the man to whom he also attributed 'mischief and wickedness'. The guiding light in all Cromwell's endeavours was the Word of God: 'I am a poor weak creature yet accepted to serve the Lord and His people.' Constant utterances of this nature give a conviction and sincerity to Cromwell's conduct which it is both unhistorical and uncharitable to reject. 'If I have innocence and integrity, the Lord hath mercy and truth and will own it.'

There were the qualities and values that sustained Cromwell in public life. In their wake lay the head of Charles, the conquest of Scotland, Irish blood and the expulsion of the Rump. They were qualities and values which dictated the course of his actions, not least the foreign policies he pursued. The cause of religion, as Cromwell understood it, was the cause of Protestantism. It was fundamental to his emotions, and instinctive to his behaviour. It was the essence of his world. It makes sense that it should have governed the course of his foreign policy: 'If you should decline this mission, the Protestant interest would suffer by it,' he said to the first ambassador he sent overseas.

Clarendon called him a man of 'private and obscure birth'. He added, in a bracket, 'though of good family'. The Cromwell family were modest country gentry. Oliver himself had known the problems of unprofitable farming, though by the time he was Protector his circumstances had improved. But of vast resources of wealth he was neither envious nor aware. Cromwell's personal protest in the Civil War had not been on economic grounds (save in the constitutional defence of property against taxation). It is therefore as unreasonable to expect a sophisticated economic approach in his foreign policy as it is reasonable to anticipate a devout religious one. The interaction of these two strands forms the substance of this and the following chapter. It seemed unlikely after the death of Charles I that the new republic would immediately formulate a policy towards Europe. Europe's own reaction was to reject it. Catholic and Protestant powers were uniformly hostile, the Russian Tsar Alexis even expelling English merchants. Exiled royalists received a welcome on the continent, Prince Rupert being particularly active against English merchant shipping at sea off Portugal and in the Mediterranean. Charles II's presence in Europe became a matter of increasing concern to the Commonwealth as the years went by. Indeed, it was in the initial defeats of Prince Rupert and of Charles that the Republic first gained a military and naval reputation. Immediately after the execution of King Charles I government in England was vested in the remaining members of the House of Commons—the survivors of the Long Parliament—and a council of state elected by them. Military order was established by Cromwell's victories in Ireland, Scotland and England, while constitutional disorder was set aside by his forcible dissolution of the Long Parliament in April 1653. Eight months later he consolidated his authority by becoming Lord Protector. From that moment when the 'Rump' were bidden to 'Go' until his death five and a half years later Oliver Cromwell dictated the course of English foreign policy.

Four European countries provide the main themes of Cromwell's foreign policy: Holland, Sweden, France and Spain. Principally Holland and Sweden occupied his attention until the autumn of 1654, when he addressed the First Protectorate Parliament on the 'Interest of the Nation'. It was a moment of triumph: 'I dare say that there is not a nation in Europe but is very willing to ask a good understanding with you.' Apart from looking ahead beyond 1654 to conclude Cromwell's Swedish policy, that is the point at which this chapter will end.

Shortly after the death of the Stadtholder William II in November 1650, the Dutch recognized the Commonwealth, in January 1651, and the English republican government responded by sending Walter Strickland and Oliver St. John to Holland, where they spent the summer of 1651. Strickland had been an agent of the Long Parliament in the Netherlands throughout the Civil War, while St. John was an experienced politician and lawyer. They were given a rough reception by the Dutch public, who hailed them as 'king-murderers', nor were the States-General enthusiastic about the purpose of their mission.

The two men had come to urge the Dutch to agree to a political union with England. The Republic's objective was fundamentally commercial. Such a union would contribute to a vast economic monopoly made up of English and Dutch home and colonial interests. The Dutch rejected the proposals, partly because of the implied threat to their economic sovereignty, and partly because—as part of the agreement—they were asked to expel exiled royalty within their borders. In consequence, at the instance of St. John, the Long Parliament passed the Navigation Act of October 1651. This famous legislative measure was as much an indiction of overall government strategy as an act directed specifically against the Dutch. In a sense, it provided the alternative diplomacy: negotiations with the Dutch had failed; legislation against them must succeed. The politicians responsible were very much concerned with the interests of trade. Thus the Navigation Act was designed to encourage the use of British or colonial shipping.[1] Only European vessels bearing goods from their own country might enter British ports. The Dutch might not be 'carriers'. Furthermore, aliens might not fish in British waters.

Dutch shipping interests were offended rather than affected. There were not enough English ships to do them out of business,

[1] Royalist interests in Virginia for example had been using Dutch ships to despatch their products.

and their government sent delegates to London, as they had done before in James I's reign, to iron out differences. They spent the first half of 1652 in England, and the proceedings clearly indicate that a strong pressure-group for peace existed in the United Provinces.

On the other hand, the Dutch were angered at the capture off Barbados of thirteen of their ships as illicit carriers.[1] Furthermore, they strongly resented the searching of their vessels for French cargoes—arising out of the Anglo-French mutual embargo on certain goods. They regarded the English claim of the right to search as a challenge to their freedom of activity on the seas, and saw no reason why bad Anglo-French relations should cause detriment to Dutch trade. In defence of their interests the Dutch decided in March 1652 'for the better guard of the sea and for the preservation and protection of navigation and commerce' to fit out 150 additional ships of war. The existence of this fleet—which increased the number of Dutch armed shipping from 76 to 226—hardened opinion in England. Its purpose was to protect Dutch merchantmen from being searched. It was the occasion of war when it became involved in the thorny issue of 'the flag'—the obligation demanded by England that her ships be saluted by foreign vessels in the Narrow Seas by the striking of the flag. A clash between the two great admirals of the time, Martin Tromp and Robert Blake, on this very issue off Dover in May 1652 provided the immediate *casus belli*. At the end of June the Dutch envoys left London and the first Anglo-Dutch War began.

It was a war for which English commercial opinion had been spoiling. Merchants and shipping magnates wanted it. The navy, especially after the voyages to the West Indies in 1650 to enforce the authority of the Commonwealth, was in trim. Lest public opinion might resent the sectional interest of the war-mongers, considerable propaganda literature was distributed which emphasized Dutch offences. On 9 July parliament published a twenty-eight thousand word pamphlet on Anglo-Dutch relations. It spoke of the 'cruel and bloody business of Amboina', of the denial of the 'usual respect to the ships of war of this nation' and the 'ready and constant help'

---

[1] Again, this illustrates that the Navigation Act was partly directed against the trade of 'royalist' colonies such as Barbados.

the Dutch had received from the English in their struggle for Independence. Not surprisingly it blamed Tromp for the engagement in May. With considerable frankness it printed the speeches of Adrian Pauw, the Dutch ambassador, who had tried hard in June to keep peace between the two nations. Pauw's appeal was partly based on the claims of unified Protestantism as well as those of mutual commercial benefit. The English Council of State doubted if Pauw really represented Dutch opinion, though the urgency of his pleas could not be doubted. Between 11 June and 30 June he made twelve separate statements to the English Council, two on the same day on 27 June. Finally on 30 June he took his leave, with a final plea for the 'mutual peace of both states'. Fundamentally, discussions had broken down because the major issues in the conflict had been by-passed by Pauw.

Indeed, these issues were such as to make resort to war inevitable sooner or later. The two sea powers were rivals 'for the fairest mistress in the world—trade'; they clashed in South America, West Africa and the Far East. There were bitter disputes between Dutch and English fishermen over the herring beds in the North Sea. The English claim to sovereignty over the Narrow Seas was resented by the Dutch, whose main trade artery was the English Channel. It was these deeper causes which led to this and two further Anglo-Dutch wars during the seventeenth century.

If opinion at large wanted a Dutch war, and saw the defeat of Dutch commercial interests as an end in itself, there were others, such as Oliver Cromwell, who felt differently. He probably accepted the need for war—he was in London during the summer of 1652 and in touch with opinion—but he wished it to terminate quickly, since he had wider visions. 'I do not like the war. I will do everything in my power to bring about peace,' he remarked, while he reminded the Dutch themselves in 1653 of the economic value of an identity of interest with the Commonwealth. Far more significantly, John Thurloe[1] tells us that Cromwell 'deplored the lamentable state of the Protestant Cause, whilst this war continues'.

Fighting during the war was mainly confined to the eighteen

[1] The role of Thurloe is mentioned at the start of the next chapter.

months from June 1652 to the end of 1653. In that period the Dutch
and English had several encounters in the Channel. Since England
flanked the Channel the Dutch were at a serious strategic disadvantage. If they lost control of their main trade route they would be
forced into submission. Hence the series of great sea battles—eight
altogether—which characterized the first Anglo-Dutch War.

Tromp, a sea-captain since the 1620s, and Blake, a soldier turned
sailor at the age of fifty, were the principal figures. Although Tromp
beat Blake off Dungeness in November 1652, Blake had already
struck the first blow the preceding May, and was to do so again at
Portland in February 1653. By the summer of 1653 the English
were in control of the war. A pamphlet, illustrated by a picture of
ships in battle, was on sale in London, describing Blake's victory over
Tromp in the battle of the Gabbard in June 1653. A Dutchman
noted the effect of the disaster: "tis here pitiful to see the amazement
among all sorts of people', while sailors were reluctant to go to sea,
'for they go not now greedily against the English, seeing they get
nothing but blows'. Even six ships intended for the East Indies were
being hastily unladen 'to be made men of war, for now all our welfare hangs upon it'. A month later the Dutch lost Tromp, in an action
in the English Channel which virtually ended the war. His death
not only deprived them of a leader of great ability, but also provoked
quarrels within the provinces as to who should succeed him, 'each
asking to have one suitable to its desire and satisfaction'. The English navy had proved technically superior to the Dutch in tactics,
size and fire-power. It had also been more effective in routine administration and in establishing the chain of command between officers.
But the real achievement of the war was not so much the prestige
victories in the Channel, but rather the capture of Dutch merchant
ships—probably well over a thousand of them—in the Baltic,
Mediterranean, East Indies and West Indies.

The Dutch might have put a fleet to sea again in 1654. Blake
was informed in March 1654 that they could raise 'a considerable
fleet very speedily', but an intercepted letter from Holland gave
the real state of affairs—'the joy here is very great, being assured of
the peace with England'. Oliver Cromwell's offer was blunt but
realistic: 'The Lord has declared against you. After the defeat you

have undergone, your only resource is to associate yourselves with your formidable neighbour,' he told them. Cromwell had become Lord Protector on 16 December 1653, installed with pomp and scarlet in Westminster Hall according to the terms of the Instrument of Government. He was in a position to create the peace which he felt was essential. The Dutch were finding potential allies in the Danes and even the French. They were more important to him as Protestant allies than commercial opponents. Terms were signed in the treaty of Westminster in April 1654.

Cromwell might have seen the Dutch as Protestant allies, but it did not stop him driving hard bargains in the peace negotiations. The clauses of the treaty of Westminster included compensation by the Dutch for damage to English merchant shipping, acquiescence in the Navigation Act and agreement to salute the British flag in certain waters. Cromwell, with more wisdom (and less ground) than the statesmen of 1919, withdrew his insistence upon payment of reparations and acknowledgement of war-guilt. Indeed, it is arguable that the war-guilt was manifestly English rather than Dutch. Three further clauses of the treaty call for particular comment. English Royalists were to be expelled from the Netherlands, while the Dutch royal house of Orange was to be excluded from holding the office of stadtholder or captain-general.[1] Together they indicate Cromwell's concern that republicanism in England should triumph. A restored Stuart was the spectre at the feast throughout his Protectorate. The authority, not to say audacity, with which Cromwell forced his policy of Orange exclusion on a reluctant States-General frightened the Dutch into submission and focused European attention on the Protector. The ultimate consequences of his secret diplomacy on the career of the new Dutch leader, John de Witt, did not matter to Cromwell. He had dismayed royalism and struck a blow for republicanism. This was clear enough: what was less evident was the illusion of a Protestant unity. The peace treaty—the first in Europe since Westphalia—was cast in the new mould of secular politics uninhibited by religious considerations. Yet for Cromwell the essence of the peace, which he expressed by singing

[1] William II's infant son, born a week after his father's death, was half-Stuart. Ultimately this child became ruler of both the Netherlands and England in 1688.

the 123rd Psalm with the Dutch envoys, was its prospect of pan-Protestantism. But to a large number of Englishmen the economic consequences of the peace were what mattered. Businessmen—with whom Cromwell never had a good relationship—had wanted the war, and guardedly accepted the peace. The merchant Slingsby Bethel—a hostile source—felt the victors did not get 'those advantages for trade' they deserved. Cromwell's problem around the negotiating table had been to reconcile his personal hopes for a Protestant alliance with the economic concessions to which his country was entitled for winning the war. He would have liked the Dutch to have declared against Catholic Spain. He offered to divide colonial spheres of interest between Dutch and English; he suggested repealing the Navigation Act. They were gestures of dubious benefit to England, but they did not come about because the Dutch were not prepared to fight Spain at Cromwell's behest. Although the settlement impressed Europe with the authority of the Protectorate, it is arguable that Cromwell won the war and lost the peace. He had put Protestantism before commerce. He had won nothing for Protestant unity and done little to allay commercial jealousy. Yet in domestic terms the treaty had some significance for the permanency of Cromwell in office. Ten days after it was signed in April 1654 he and his family moved into Whitehall Palace. The Cromwells had come to stay.

Cromwell's Dutch policy must not be seen in isolation. Closely related to his discussions with the Dutch envoys were the ones being simultaneously conducted on his behalf with Sweden. Once again, religious and commercial issues were at stake.

THE SWEDES

On that same December day in 1653 on which Oliver Cromwell was installed as Protector, a middle-aged Englishman who had reluctantly left a wife nearing confinement, was journeying by coach over ice towards the Swedish town of Uppsala. Bulstrode Whitelocke was a lawyer of independent mind. He had taken no part in the condemnation of Charles I, and had subsequently suggested to Cromwell that he should negotiate with Charles II. Nevertheless, he was chosen by Cromwell to be the first ambassador of the Commonwealth, charged with presenting himself at the court of Queen Christina of Sweden—to whom Cromwell had already sent the gift of his own portrait. Whitelocke was instructed to bring the two nations into 'nearer union and correspondence with respect to the common interest of the true Protestant religion'. He was also expected to secure Swedish influence in negotiating 'a free trade through the Sound; that it may not depend upon the will of the king of Denmark, or the United Provinces of the Netherlands'. The Sound was the narrow strait of water between Sweden and the Danish island of Zealand which permitted a passage into the Baltic. From the twelfth century onwards it had had strategic and commercial importance in the rivalries of the Scandinavian countries, the Hanseatic League, the Low Countries and England. Denmark had levied duties on ships (from 1429) and on their cargoes (from 1567), making such concessions as she thought fit. Sweden had obtained exemption in 1613, and the Dutch had compounded for a lump sum in 1649.[1]

English merchants needed Baltic trade in timber, tar and wheat. Whitelocke stayed in Sweden for five months and created a favourable impression on Christina, besides arousing some envy, mixed with respect, amongst other ambassadors. In a revealing passage the Dutch ambassador, Conrad Van Beuningen, reported home in January 1654 that Whitelocke had been boasting of the English shipbuilding programme. 'If you have any advice of the contrary, your lordships may please to signify so much unto me, that I may confute him.' In other words, Whitelocke was carrying out a successful public relations exercise for his country. As we have seen, the Dutch States-General would have been able to give Van Beuningen little assurance of their own naval strength with which to answer Whitelocke back. By the end of April 1654 the terms of a commercial treaty had been agreed. English access to the Sound, and to Baltic trade, was permitted, while another clause allowed each to carry on mutual trade with each other's enemy in time of war—except for contraband.

Beyond a brief reference to the common bond of Protestantism,

---

[1] Dues were finally ended in 1857.

no mention was made of religion in the treaty. There might have been more chance if Axel Oxenstierna, Christina's elderly minister, had played a larger part in the discussions.[1] He represented a tradition that looked backwards to the significance of religion in political alignments. Younger Swedish diplomats, such as John Salvius, rejected mutual Protestantism as a basis for agreements in favour of a more secular foreign policy. Christina herself took a cynical view. Although she excused Cromwell and Whitelocke from her accusations, she declared that the English used religion as a means of obtaining alliances that had commercial value; 'there are many who make profession of more holiness than is in them, hoping for advantage by it'. Whitelocke's success in the clauses on the Sound was given more substance by the treaty Cromwell made later in the summer with Denmark.[2] Denmark not only lay on one side of the Sound, but also owned in Scania a narrow strip of Sweden's southern coastline, and commanded the entrance to the Sound.

To add to the Swedish and Danish treaties, Cromwell had his peace with the Dutch, together with a treaty with Portugal in July 1654 giving the English the right of commerce in Portuguese colonies without religious interference. Anglo-Portuguese relations, normally happy, had suffered when Lisbon became a base for Prince Rupert and other exiled royalists. By the autumn of 1654, therefore, Cromwell had negotiated successfully with several European countries and always obtained terms in his favour.

This is the point at which we may notice his own appraisal of his achievements abroad. He never forgot the significance of 3 September, and on that date—four years after Dunbar—article 7 of the Instruments of Government required the first Protectorate Parliament to meet.[3] The occasion was marked with ceremony: Cromwell arrived in state, attended by Life-Guards and 'pages and laqueys

---

[1] Oxenstierna and Whitelocke got on well, although the Swedish statesman had grave doubts about the validity of Cromwell's authority.

[2] The treaty was made in July but not finally ratified till September—after Cromwell's speech to the first Protectorate Parliament.

[3] 3 September was a Sunday. MP's heard a sermon in the Abbey and a brief speech from Cromwell at five o'clock in which he indicated that his main speech would be given next morning.

richly clothed', although, as a French observer noticed, Cromwell himself was 'very modestly clothed'. Bulstrode Whitelocke, very much in favour, carried the purse and tells us that Cromwell made 'a large and subtle speech'. He described the Dutch treaty as one of great benefit, emphasizing his own concern for peace with a Protestant state. There was significantly no mention of commercial advantages won from the Dutch in the treaty of Westminster. He attributed 'an honourable' agreement with Sweden to the work of Whitelocke and repeated the virtues of 'a good understanding with Protestant friends'. He saw the real value of the Danish treaty in guaranteeing the opening of the Sound to English commerce. The nation could trade direct with the Baltic with 'as much freedom as the Dutch themselves and at the same rates and toll'. Finally, he welcomed the peace with Portugal—a peace which 'merchants make us believe is of good concernement to their trade', and which gives 'liberty of conscience' to our people. A long speech, which had placed the religious interests of the Commonwealth before its secular ones, ended with an apology for being tedious— 'but I did judge that it was somewhat necessary to acquaint you with these things'. Clearly Cromwell saw Baltic affairs rather than Dutch ones as representing the greater triumph in diplomacy. Yet in his policies during the next four years the Baltic played less part than might have been expected. For instance, on no occasion did he take the initiative in Anglo-Swedish diplomacy. Nor did Sweden's new King, Charles X, keep to the path of the Protestant interest as scrupulously as Cromwell would have liked. Charles X, who succeeded Christina on her abdication in 1654, brought Swedish power to its zenith in a brief reign of six years. In his attempt to consolidate Swedish control of the Baltic he fought variously against Poles, Russians, Danes, Dutch, Brandenburg, and the Empire. Every power with a stake in the Baltic was his enemy at one time or another. But Charles X's policies had not been possible without external support. On one occasion it came from Brandenburg with whom, by 1657, he was at war; twice it was sought from Cromwell. Cromwell certainly retained his interest in Sweden, and he still contemplated a realistic Protestant alliance in which Sweden might fight with England against the Catholic Habsburgs. But it was a policy irrelevant to the pursuits of Charles X. The Protector was only useful to Charles in military terms. Charles's first approach to Cromwell was in 1655, for help in the Baltic against the Dutch. Dutch trading interests were threatened by Charles's policies and they had resisted him in several ways. Cromwell was caught squarely between two fires—either he helped Sweden, and abandoned a Protestant alliance with the Dutch, or he helped the Dutch to minimize Swedish power in the Baltic and protected English commercial interests at the price of playing second fiddle to Holland. Whitelocke urged him to help Sweden in return for the guarantee of the monopoly of Swedish copper sales. In the end the pro-Dutch group in the Council triumphed, and Cromwell did nothing beyond allowing Sweden to raise a specified number of volunteers in England in return for trade concessions at Swedish ports in the Baltic.

Two years later Charles X was challenged by Russians, Poles, Danes and Dutch, and for a time was in serious trouble. Consequently negotiations again took place between Charles and Cromwell. Charles wanted ships and money: Cromwell was prepared to offer these—and had twenty ships got ready—in return for the mortgaging to England of Bremen as a continental base for North German trade. Again, nothing came of these plans.[1] Cromwell was heavily committed in the Spanish war; Bremen was too expensive; nor indeed was Cromwell entirely persuaded of the virtue of Sweden's cause. He informed the Danes, through his ambassador Philip Meadows, that he hoped the war would end. Swedish domination of the Baltic did not seem in Europe's interest. The time was past, Cromwell noted (wrongly), when 'one kingdom might swallow up another'. He welcomed the peace which Denmark and Sweden made at Roeskilde in February 1658. In the summer war broke out again in the North. Cromwell was concerned at the continuing power of Sweden, and felt it a threat to Baltic interests. But the prior commitment of war with Spain, and his own declining health, prevented anything being done before his death in September 1658. His Baltic policy, begun with such promise, fundamentally failed because, as Whitelocke himself saw, it was identified with a Protes-

---

[1] Cromwell could not afford the mortgage anyway in 1658.

tantism which Charles X took lightly. Cromwell's hopes for a coalition of Sweden, Holland, Denmark and Brandenburg against Catholic Austria had no meaning for Charles X, to whom the Baltic conflict was one for economic gain. The settlements made in 1660-1 defined power-politics in the Baltic for the rest of the century: Sweden triumphed, Brandenburg rose, Denmark made concessions and Poland declined. No one was really interested in that campaign against the Habsburgs after which Cromwell had always hankered.

By 3 September 1654 Cromwell had accomplished a great deal in a short time. He had made alliances and treaties with several European powers; sometimes ones which were in conflict with each other. Furthermore, he had established the reputation of the Commonwealth in a way more effective than naked force. In Whitelocke he had chosen his first overseas representative. Whitelocke, suspicious of why he was asked to go to Sweden and wondering if he was being got out of the way, was just the right man to restore respect for England. Cromwell was concerned that other nations should no longer think of it as a land of 'king-murderers'. In selecting Whitelocke Cromwell told him, 'You are the fittest man in the nation for this service; we know your abilities; we know you have languages and have travelled, and understand the interest of Christendom. We know you to be a gentleman of good family, related to persons of honour.' Away from the mainstream of European intrigue Whitelocke displayed for the benefit of other attendant ambassadors the conservatism of the new régime in England. Seven years later, at the Restoration, Whitelocke's moderate outlook saved him, and he went into dignified retirement from public life. By 1654 his part in public life had contributed to the greatness of Cromwell abroad.

7 Cromwell: the French and the Spanish, 1654–60

> Those who have an intimate acquaintance with affairs here think that the war with the Spaniards will bring great harm to England
>
> *Giovanni Sagredo, the Venetian ambassador*

THE FRENCH

Bulstrode Whitelocke's appointment had been an example of Cromwell's policy of 'choosing men for places, and not places for men'. The author of that remark was John Thurloe, a lawyer who had first served the Republic in 1651 as St. John's secretary in the United Provinces. In the following year he became secretary to the Council of State and clerk to the committee for foreign affairs. Cromwell co-opted him to membership of the Council of State, and a close association between the two men began. Thurloe is important for four reasons. He was in charge of the intelligence department under the Council of State. In this post he handled the receipt and distribution of all diplomatic correspondence and knew more than anyone else what was the temper of European opinion on matters vital to government foreign policy. Secondly, he was an extremely efficient administrator, who worked with the impartiality of a civil servant—his services were briefly used at the Restoration by Clarendon. Thirdly, he was someone with whom Cromwell could discuss affairs of state—'laying aside his greatness (Cromwell) would be exceeding familiar'. We owe this information to Whitelocke. With both Thurloe and Whitelocke, Cromwell would be 'shut up three or four hours together in private discourse'. All great men need their confidants, though they usually make their own decisions in the end. This was true of Cromwell's relationship with

Thurloe, who told him a great deal, but who did not have much influence on his policies. Fourthly, the historian of the Cromwellian period has a vast source of material in Thurloe's collected papers at the Bodleian Library in Oxford.

Surveying the political scene in 1654, Thurloe observed: 'The French are anxious to conclude a treaty with his Highness. The Spanish hope is to win him to their side.' It is the relationship of Cromwell with those two nations which forms the subject of this chapter.

Relations between England and France had been cool from the moment of Charles's execution. Mazarin feared, as we saw in chapter 4, the greater strength of the republic at sea, and demonstrated his hostility by putting an embargo on English draperies. The English replied by banning French wines and silks, and the privateers of both countries profited accordingly by illicit attacks on each other. Indeed, Dutch resentment at searching of their ships for French goods was a major factor in the outbreak of war in 1652. Unofficial warfare at sea continued during the official Dutch conflict. Only towards the end of that war did the French, as Thuloe observed, come to favour the prospect of an alliance. Mazarin decided that he must come to terms with the Commonwealth, dispatching at the end of 1652 an envoy, Antoine de Bordeaux, to watch developments. Bordeaux was left in no doubt as to what Cromwell thought of him. 'For some time, Mr. Cromwell has informed me', he wrote back to Paris on 23 October 1653, 'that he wishes me no longer to address myself to him about matters of business, and he has even avoided me on several occasions. I have been unable to converse with him.' In the spring of 1654 Mazarin was trying every sort of flattery, raising Bordeaux to the rank of an ambassador, finding out if Cromwell would like Louis XIV to address him as '*Mon cousin*',[1] offering cash and Dunkirk—when it was back in French hands. He tacitly accepted Cromwell's indefensible action of occupying Nova Scotia in the summer of 1654.[2] But Cromwell procrastinated. Not

---

[1] Louis drew the line at '*Mon frère*' and Cromwell in any case preferred and chose '*Monsieur le Protecteur*'.

[2] An expedition sent against the Dutch settlements in North America was redirected to Nova Scotia after the signing of peace between England and the United Provinces.

until October 1655 was Bordeaux rewarded, when a commercial treaty was made with France. 'If it had lost its gracefulness by its long postponement', Bordeaux reported, 'it would seem that the rupture with Spain is likely to lend it new charms.'

In reaching this arrangement with France Cromwell finally committed himself to a pro-French and anti-Spanish policy. He had had to contend with divided opinion in the Council of State. Those who leant towards Spain used such arguments as the association of France with Royalist exiles and the attacks on English commerce. They were in a minority compared to the advocates of the traditional anti-Spanish attitude, who visualized the advantages of attacks on Spanish commerce, 'the most profitable of any in the world'. By the time that Cromwell met his first Protectorate parliament, in September 1654, he at least knew the course of action upon which he had determined. But the French had to wait throughout most of 1655 for the confirmation of their treaty, owing to an incident in Savoy. The Protestants dwelling there, known as the Vaudois, were being intimidated by military force wielded by the French government to become Catholics. Cromwell, by diplomacy rather than counter-force, caused Mazarin to call off the campaign and leave the Vaudois to their Protestantism.[1] But the commercial alliance finally came in November, proclaimed by 'heralds and trumpets'. At this point, Cromwell was not in such a strong position as he had been a few months earlier. His campaign in the Spanish Indies had failed, as we shall see later in the chapter.

Cromwell's interest in France included the prospect of securing Dunkirk. Dunkirk was the most northerly French seaport, bordering on the Spanish Netherlands, and with strategic and commercial importance going back to the Middle Ages. The Council of State, somewhat foolishly, had let it fall into Spanish hands in 1652, when Mazarin had refused to bargain over it. By 1657 Cromwell wanted it more than ever. and its ultimate cession to England was the major plank of the military alliance between the two countries finally agreed in March 1657.

---

[1] Cromwell's Protestant conscience was deeply concerned. He gave £2000 to the relief fund for those who had suffered in the affair. It was a very large sum in relation to his financial resources.

The alliance owed much to the work of Sir William Lockhart, a thirty-six year old soldier whom Charles I had knighted and whom Cromwell had sent back to his Scots homeland as a commissioner for the administration of justice.[1] Lockhart was sent to France as ambassador in 1656. He was a man who did 'diplomatic, warlike and whatever work' came before him 'in an effectual and manful manner'. Since the clauses of the treaty were closely bound up with Cromwell's policy towards Spain, this is a convenient place for us to consider Anglo-Spanish relations, from the moment when the Protectorate was recognized by Spain in December 1650 until the Spanish themselves experienced the implications of the treaty with France, which Cromwell had made 'for assaulting the Spanish power in the Netherlands'. Spain had shared in the general hostility to the Commonwealth, but less emphatically than other nations. She rejected a petition for help from Charles II, although doing little to avenge the murder by exiled royalists in Madrid of a Commonwealth representative. Political factors governed Spanish attitudes towards England. While France and Spain remained at war—as they did for eleven years after Westphalia—neither wished Cromwell to join the other. Spanish ministers were ready to go far to secure Cromwell's alliance against France, but they failed to make allowance for the real objectives in Cromwell's mind. For him an anti-Spanish policy was an alternative expression of his deep belief in a Protestant foreign policy. If commercial aspects were to be almost as important, this was but a collective reflection of the hostility of English Protestantism to Spanish wealth as much as Spanish religion. But Cromwell's initial approach to his two suitors—French and Spanish—was realistic and nationalistic. He would endeavour to secure the best bargain for England which diplomacy could achieve.

From Spain he wanted money to finance an anti-French campaign. He also sought freedom of trade in the Indies, so that Englishmen might move unhindered by the double stigma of being both heretics and interlopers. To ask this, exclaimed the Spanish ambassador in

[1] He married Cromwell's niece, though this connection would only have pleased the Protector—not influenced him.

London, Alonso de Cardenas, was to ask for his 'master's two eyes'. 'Nothing can be done in this respect,' Cardenas replied. The break-down of negotiations with Spain was final and led Cromwell to fall in line with majority opinion in the Council of State and implement an anti-Spanish campaign.

THE SPANISH

Already, in July 1654, a Mediterranean voyage by Blake, to defend English commercial interests against Algiers, had provided a display of strength calculated to impress the French. The Dey of Algiers was forced to release English prisoners and concede freedom of trade to English merchants. In April 1655 Blake destroyed the fleet of the Dey of Tunis. These two successes not only taught the Barbary pirates an effective lesson, but were also an indication to Europe as a whole that Cromwell had a long arm. The experience of this expedition convinced Cromwell that his navy could under-take the real task he had in mind—a campaign in the West Indies. Late in August 1654 instructions were given to get the fleet ready. When Cromwell addressed the Protectorate parliament on 4 September on the virtues of peace, he naturally made no mention of this next phase of his foreign policy. Only a guarded hint that he believed that they would 'not expect much good from Catholic neighbours' might have been taken as an indication of an aggressive new anti-Spanish policy.

The commander-in-chief of the expedition, which finally sailed for the West Indies in December 1654, leaving a chilly English climate for the tropical sun of Barbados, was Admiral William Penn. With him went General Robert Venables. Penn's commission required him to establish a firm footing 'in that part of the West Indies in the possession of the Spaniard'. This was clearly a challenge wedded to history. The Spanish monopolist claims—sustained since the days of the treaty of Tordesillas and not conceded in the treaty of London—were to be called in question. Cromwell, in common with so many of his contemporaries, nursed a grievance against the Spanish for their arrogance towards England. As a young student in London he might have been up early enough in the morning to see the execution of Sir Walter Raleigh at eight a.m. on 29 October

1618.[1] Raleigh's death, at the instigation of the Spanish ambassador, was one score to be settled. Furthermore, in Raleigh's life there was much to inspire Cromwellian imperial objectives.

The expedition of Penn and Venables was not a success, though its failure should be tempered by a recognition of the great issues at stake. It was a combined naval–military operation under commanders who had little idea of how to co-operate. After recruiting and watering at Barbados, an attempt to take San Domingo in Hispaniola failed for a variety of reasons: parched throats and dysentery; successful Spanish ambushes; ill-trained 'pressed' troops from Barbados. Rather than return empty-handed, Penn and Venables made the random decision to capture Jamaica. In this they succeeded, but the ultimate significance of Jamaica as a British possession could not then be gauged. They returned to disgrace and brief imprisonment. Meanwhile, a second naval expedition under Blake, had been dispatched in March 1655, while the first one was approaching Hispaniola. Blake's instructions required him to intercept Spanish shipping sailing to the Indies and capture the returning treasure-fleet. Outgoing shipping was for the moment prevented from going to the Indies, but no fleet was captured. But Blake could not be accused of culpable failure as could Penn and Venables, neither of whom had been completely trusted by Cromwell.[2] We need to look further than lack of trust or confidence to explain Cromwell's harshness towards them.

Several explanations may be offered. Cromwell, who prided himself on military success, had tasted defeat—Jamaica, a poor place full of wild cattle, was no recompense. Secondly, his policies had failed at a time when he was surrounded by enemies—there had been a rash of minor conspiracies in the spring of 1655 inspired by Royalist factions. Thirdly, the Protectorate was in some financial trouble, which successful action in the West Indies might have

[1] Cromwell was probably studying law privately. His name appears on no Inns of Court list. Raleigh's execution, so early on an autumn morning, supports the view that James I knew he was requiring a distasteful act. But it did not stop a large crowd attending.

[2] Subsequently Penn lived on the continent, became a royalist, and served the navy in Charles II's reign.

alleviated—Drake had been knighted in 1581 as much for the money he brought back as for the prestige he had won. Fourthly, the setback meant that Cromwell—who had cast the dice against Spain, with nothing to show for it—could no longer treat Mazarin's approaches for an alliance with such disdain. Mazarin duly got his alliance—if only a commercial one—in October 1655. Fifthly, the merchant classes felt severely the impact of the Spanish reprisal, an embargo on English ships in Spanish ports. This meant that Englishmen could not export cloth, manufactured goods and Newfoundland cod to Spain herself. Not only did the suppliers of these commodities suffer, but also shipbuilders. The Dutch were quick to take advantage —both as carriers and as cloth manufacturers. Contemporary criticism was bitter and Cromwell was even less in favour with the London 'city' interests. But the sixth and most important explanation was the basic failure of the economic aspect of Cromwell's foreign policy. His instructions to Blake in the second expedition emphasize his concern for a campaign to bring the 'true religion into those parts' as well as gain an economic foothold which could be the basis of future settlements. It is this that gives meaning to Cromwell's 'Western Design'. It was intended to express his belief in Protestantism and yet recognize the country's economic ambitions. Cromwell, who had become friendly with a London businessman, Maurice Thompson, was able to match his own preferences with Thompson's advice on the economics of West Indian settlement. Another way of looking at the 'Western Design' is to consider Cromwell as selecting an aspect of Elizabethan foreign policy and giving it reality. Elizabethans, particularly those concerned about over-population, unemployment and redundancy, had visualized settlement and colonization as a solution to these problems. Under the first two Stuarts much of this had gone to the Americas. Those who doubted the durability of the English East India Company saw an alternative prospect in the West Indies.

But there could be no turning back. Spain withdrew her ambassador and regarded herself at war with England. Cromwell determined that Jamaica, better placed strategically than Barbados, would be the foundation of an English imperial interest in the Caribbean. He dispatched letters to Admiral William Goodson and General

Richard Fortescue, both of whom Penn had left behind in Jamaica, and to Daniel Serle, the Governor of Barbados. They were told to prepare 'to beat the Spaniard, who will doubtless send a good force to the Indies'.[1] Troops were promised, from both the New England colonies and the British Isles, as well as 'seven more stout men of war, some of them forty guns'. Serle was reminded that the campaign had a religious basis, 'and therefore we dare not relinquish it'. In a sense, Cromwell now needed all the courage of his convictions. His 'Western Design', which he described to Serle as having miscarried 'through the disposing hand of God', had to be converted into something concrete and tangible in result. The winter of 1655–6 was not without its troubles.[2] What was needed was commercial gain from the war: what happened during that winter was a series of financial problems for Cromwell in financing war with Spain. In December 1655 he readmitted the Jews to England, finance being among his motives. The Stuarts' perennial problem had become that of Cromwell too. Briefly, it led him to hold a general election, in order that the parliament he faced in September 1656 should give a sympathetic ear to his statement of war-policy. Cromwell's speech to the second Protectorate parliament was twenty thousand words in length—sixty pages of this book. He opened by saying, 'So far as possible, on this large subject, let us be brief; not studying the art of rhetoricians'. After seventeen thousand words he remarked, 'I have little more to say to you, being very weary; and I know you are too'. Moments later, he added: 'I have but one thing more to say. I know it is troublesome, but I did read a Psalm yesterday, which truly may not unbecome both me to tell you of, and you to observe.' Finally, after reading and discussing the Psalm—the 85th—he ends, 'I have done'. The speech was twice as long as the one in which Cromwell had addressed the first Protectorate parliament on its first

---

[1] Fortescue never got his letter. He died in October 1655.

[2] This passage from a letter from Henriette Maria to Charles II, written on Christmas Eve 1655, is of interest in this respect:

Pour moy, je ne puis comprandre, que les Espagnols ayant rien à menager du côté de Cromwell: car certainement il est résolu de les ruiner; ils n'ont rien à faire qu'a se joindre avec vous.

G

meeting. He had both to justify the war with Spain and win financial support for its continuance.

His audience was not necessarily friendly, and after his speech was over the Council of State invalidated the return to parliament of nearly a hundred of its members. The rule of the major-generals was unattractive to the country, and much of the parliamentary representation from the south-east of England was openly hostile to the Protectorate. Those who were allowed to stay for the further proceedings of the House were to be involved the following March in offering Cromwell the crown. The speech itself outlined the dangers which the Protectorate faced from its enemies both at home and abroad; Cromwell was acutely aware of royalist moves to restore Charles II. But his main theme was that of the historic threat of Spain, a 'natural enemy' who had tried 'to destroy Elizabeth of famous memory', and had denied Englishmen liberty of conscience in their trading activities. Conflict with Spain meant solidarity among the Protestant nations, whose 'interests in Christendom are the same as yours', and hostility to the Pope—'a person of zeal for his religion—wherein perhaps he may shame us'. Cromwell saw the new Pope Alexander VII (who had been elected in 1655) as endeavouring to unite all 'Popish interests against this nation above any, and against all the Protestant interest in the world'. Having said all this, Cromwell declared himself for toleration and this allowed him to say that France stood apart from 'a tie to the Pope'.

It was a speech constantly stressing the religious rather than the commercial significance of Cromwell's foreign policy. The Protector got the support he sought from his purged parliament and the money with which to prosecute the war. Meanwhile, the news of Admiral Richard Stayner's capture of a Spanish treasure-fleet came just at the right time. The treasury was relieved by the arrival of nearly forty wagonloads of bullion, which was at once coined.

A parliamentary session which had opened in September 1656 with the Protector on the defensive ended the following spring with Cromwell more firmly entrenched than ever. He had frustrated his enemies by turning down the offer of the throne. His ships had spent the winter blockading the Spanish coast. Blake's career was to culminate in the sinking of another treasure-fleet at Teneriffe in the

Canary Islands in April 1657. During that winter Mazarin and Cromwell had been in direct correspondence, which led to the military treaty of March 1657, which brought both powers together in a common assault upon Spain. The individual wars which each had waged were now merged into a campaign which was to outlast the Protector's life and be central to the foreign policy of his remaining eighteen months. By the terms of the treaty the English were to provide 6000 troops to assist the French in an attack on the Spanish Netherlands, primarily to secure the harbours of Gravelines (for the French) and Dunkirk and Mardyke (for the English). Both sides were making concessions: the French in allowing the prospect of an English base on their northern coastline, the English in recognizing the possibility of French strength in the Netherlands. By October English and French troops had taken Mardyke, but it was a victory of no great significance. In the following spring the campaign was renewed. In an engagement on the Dunes east of Dunkirk fought in June 1658, on the same coastline from which the British Expeditionary Force made its retreat in 1940, the French under Turenne and the English under Lockhart—ambassador and soldier—defeated Spanish forces under Don John of Austria, the Prince of Condé and James, Duke of York.

It was an epic encounter. In Turenne and Condé, old soldiers came face to face; royalist exiles fought men of the Protectorate; Dunkirk fell. Lockhart received the keys of the harbour-town from Louis XIV in person, giving to Cromwell, in the words of Thurloe, 'the keys of a door into the continent'. 'The Cardinal seems as glad to give this place to his Highness', Lockhart reported, 'as I can be to receive it.' In winning an entry into Europe Cromwell pleased the commercial classes, by ridding the ports of privateers who attacked English shipping. He also deprived the royalists of a harbour from which to launch an invasion.

THE PROTECTOR'S ACHIEVEMENT

Invasion indeed seemed a constant threat to Cromwell's position in the closing months of his life. Lockhart had informed him in February 1658 that Charles II planned to invade with four thousand troops, and Cromwell told the second Protectorate parliament that 'the king of Scots hath an army at the water's side, ready to be shipped for England. And while it is doing, there are endeavours from some who are not far from this place, to stir up the people of this town into a tumulting.' These were almost the last words Cromwell ever addressed to his parliament. A few moments later he dissolved an assembly which had proved less interested in the great issues of foreign policy than Cromwell had wished, and more concerned with 'petty quarrelling' at a time when invasion threatened. Something of the vicissitudes of the closing months of Oliver Cromwell's life emerge if we contrast the triumph of Dunkirk with the execution on Tower Hill of Sir Henry Slingsby, a connection of Cromwell's by marriage, whose royalist plotting cost him his life; or the contrast between the nephews of Mazarin coming to England to congratulate Cromwell over Dunkirk, while internal divisions led men like Charles Fleetwood and Arthur Hesilrige to desert him. But triumph and disaster in public life took second place to the private grief which engulfed Oliver as his daughter, Elizabeth, lay dying at Hampton Court. On 3 September 1658 he too was dead. His son Richard Cromwell was not the man to perpetuate a Cromwellian dynasty. The crowd in history, fickle in its loyalties, gazed at Oliver's funeral effigy in Westminster in 1658 and rejoiced at the dishonouring of his body at Tyburn in 1661. Charles II had come home.

Cromwell had come to power at the age of fifty-five. He was dead at fifty-nine. It is reasonable, even in the context of seventeenth-century life-spans, to regard his work as unfinished.[1] At home the shadows were closing in at his death. Plotting he was used to; but his financial embarrassment was getting worse. He lacked the confidence of the City of London, which never gave him a loan. 'The great want is money which puts us to the wall in all our business,' Thurloe confessed in March 1658. What fundamentally was that 'business' intended to be? To crusade for Protestantism abroad had been the perpetual objective. It seemed to have a fair

---

[1] So many politicians in the sixteenth and seventeenth centuries were not allowed, by the axe, to finish their normal life-spans, that is is difficult to suggest what might have been a reasonable expectation of life for public figures. Two who led busy lives and died natural deaths were Burghley (78) and Danby (81).

prospect of success in 1654. By 1658 the way ahead was less clear. Cromwell had made a 'Catholic' ally in France, which was shortly to make a peace treaty with Spain[1] ignoring the issues on which England had gone to war. His hopes for a base in Europe from which to conduct an anti-Habsburg campaign were short-lived. Dunkirk soon returned to France, and his motives for such a campaign had no appeal for powers such as Sweden, France or even his fellow-Englishmen. 'The Emperor hath enough to do to defend himself against the Turk,' said Henry Neville during the Protectorate of Richard.

If the crusade for Protestantism was a failure, how did that affect other aspects of Cromwell's foreign policy? He was never unaware of the economic needs of the nation, and in particular of the importance of the navy. 'The basis of English greatness', said Thomas Sprat,[2] 'lay in strength at sea.' Here Cromwell's policies endured. The Navigation Act was re-enacted at the Restoration; sea-power mattered in the decades that followed. But the merchants, who had distrusted Cromwell from the start, were reluctant to see virtues in his commercial policy, while appreciating that he strove to ensure a passage for Baltic trade. They were less happy about his conduct of Anglo-Dutch relations. Thurloe speaks for them when he tells us that the Dutch 'swallowed all' while England made war against Spain. The Spanish war brought them no effective returns in Cromwell's lifetime. Instead, it affected trade and was, said Samuel Lambe in 1659, the main reason for its unfavourable balance.

Indeed, it is the 'Western Design' that represents the unfinished area of Cromwellian foreign policy. If we say that it ultimately led to the consolidation of an English empire in the New World, with its self-sufficient economic nexus; its sugar prosperity based on slavery; and its rejection of a Spanish monopoly, then we may give Cromwell the credit for a vision of empire. But none of this was evident at his death. Cromwell knew his priorities, and never deviated from them. God's claims were greater than those of

---

[1] Peace of the Pyrenees, 1659.

[2] Sprat managed to tread the ecclesiastical tight-rope successfully, from the day he took his Oxford MA in 1657 till his participation in the coronation of William and Mary as a bishop.

Mammon. But, like the Portuguese explorer who cried 'Christians and spices', he found room for both. 'Protestants and products' would be a fair epitaph on his foreign policy, but an insufficient one.

'Prestige' must complete the alliteration: the prestige won for a nation which could turn 'to some gigantic undertaking of great advantage and detrimental to all monarchies'; the prestige which 'made all neighbouring princes fear him'. So had the Venetian ambassador remarked of him at the start, and Samuel Pepys at the end. No wonder Sir William Lockhart, who continued as England's ambassador in France after the Restoration, noted that men now showed him less respect. There could be no replacement for the greatest Englishman of his age.

8 Restoration policies, 1660–67

> I went, and one of the king's footmen, and a dog that the
> king loved, in a boat by ourselves, and so got on shore when
> the king did, who was received by General Monk with all
> imaginable love and respect at his entrance upon the land of
> Dover. Infinite the crowd of people and the horsemen,
> citizens and noblemen of all sorts
>
> *Samuel Pepys*

MARRIAGE PROPOSITIONS

Charles II was enthusiastically received at Dover on 26 May
1660. It was Samuel Pepys's first opportunity to report a great
occasion and he noted the 'shouting and joy beyond all imagination'. Charles himself was 'stunned with the acclamation of the
people', while that other diarist Evelyn rejoiced at a Restoration
unparalled 'since the return of the Jews from the Babylonish cap-
tivity'. It was essentially a domestic event, inviting so far as possible
a return to past traditions. Charles's Restoration owed nothing
to any foreign power and he was transformed from a lowly exile
into an exalted monarch by virtue of the decision of the Convention
Parliament—which had sent him £50,000 in gold for travelling
expenses. He was a man of thirty,[1] whose long years in Europe had
given him a wanderer's knowledge of its geography, a marked sympathy with Catholicism, a taste for women, and the experience of
poverty and hardship. As a bystander on the perimeter of great
affairs he had learnt to judge men. He had not had access to a kingly
association with diplomacy at the centre. His approach to his erst-
while European neighbours was open-ended. He awaited their
suits.

[1] On 29 May.

Most of Europe now took an interest in the bachelor-king and their suits were marriage ones. Spain, France, Holland and Portugal were the countries around which the foreign policy of the Restoration was centred.

At Charles's accession England was at war with Spain. A formal peace with that nation, in September 1660, was the first positive act of his foreign policy. It was made retrospective to Charles's arrival in England. Charles's proclamation of peace gave validity to the peaceful state of affairs which was actually existing between the two countries. No troops or ships were afoot. But the formal peace was less significant than the informal hostility towards the Spanish which the king himself retained.

On the face of it this is surprising. Spain had been kinder to Charles than France in his exile. Yet it was a hostility that Charles's English subjects might have been expected to welcome. It was in the tradition of seventeenth-century commercial opinion. In the end it did Charles no good. In the 1660s Spain's decline was patently evident, and she presented no menace to English interests. Englishmen in Charles II's reign preferred Spaniards to Frenchmen. An incident involving the relative precedence of the French and Spanish ambassadors, on the occasion of the arrival of the Swedish ambassador in September 1661, received a lot of publicity. The affair was stage-managed by the two embassies. Pepys of course was watching and noted that 'all the city did rejoice' at French discomfiture. 'Indeed we do naturally love the Spaniard and hate the French,' he recorded in his Diary. It was an attitude of mind in direct relationship to the threat those nations represented to English interests. No one feared the Spanish any more: their empire had been violated and their treasure spoilt.

Spanish suggestions of a bride came to nothing. There were faults on both sides. There were too many memories of the 1620s. Furthermore, the situation was entirely different from beforehand; for Spain would at this time gladly have agreed to a marriage alliance with England, but had neither territory nor money to offer. Her contribution to Charles's domestic plans proved to be the negative one of trying to prevent the eventual Portuguese marriage.

The Dutch proposed an alliance as early as July 1660, but were

dismayed by Charles's prompt demand for money and by the re-
newal of the English Navigation Act of 1651. The Dutch had refused to surrender the spice island of Poele-Rum, as promised in
1654, and relations between the English and Dutch East India Companies had grown worse. The Dutch were determined to keep the
English out of the Spice Islands, and this rivalry was soon extended
to West Africa. Sir George Downing, the ambassador at The Hague,
was against the idea of a marriage alliance, so nothing came of proposals to unite Charles with a daughter of Frederick Henry, the
stadtholder of Charles I's time.

French diplomats had been as keen as Spanish ones to approach
Charles in the halcyon summer of 1660. Despite the fact that
Cromwell and Mazarin had reached a good understanding, the
cardinal and his master, Louis XIV, now saw the value of an
alliance with the restored Stuarts; for such an alliance would en-
able Louis to strike at his chief opponent, Spain.

In the peace of the Pyrenees (1659) France had ended her war with
Spain. She gained some territorial interests in Flanders and a Spanish
wife for Louis. The settlement was strongly tilted in France's favour,
and made her the dominant power in western Europe. Nevertheless,
she was still surrounded by Spanish and Austrian Habsburg interests
and felt that Paris lay too close to alien north-eastern borders for
safety.

Mazarin, whose day was nearly done, urged Louis to 'create a
community of interests between the two states so far as should be
humanly possible', and he hoped it might be achieved by a marriage
alliance.

One possibility was Mazarin's niece, Hortense Mancini. The
cardinal had opposed such a union when Charles was an impoverished exile. Now that he was king, matters were different. In the
autumn of 1660 Queen Henrietta Maria visited England and
encouraged the match, emphasizing to her son the large dowry
Mazarin's niece would bring; yet in the end no marriage took
place. Clarendon was against it, and Charles's mother had pushed
her son too hard. Instead Anglo-French relations were strengthened
by a different marriage alliance. Charles gave his consent to a union
between his sister Henriette-Anne and the King of France's brother

Philip, Duke of Orleans. Up to a point, the marriage was a love
match—though it turned out to be a tragic and unhappy union—
and had been sought by Philip before the Restoration. It eventually
took place in March 1661, and has its own importance in foreign
affairs during the nine following years until Henriette-Anne's death.
Henriette-Anne, always known as Madame, was devoted to her
brother Charles, who once wrote to her: 'We shall never have
any other quarrel but as to which of us shall love the other most,
but in this I will never yield to you!' In a man whose relationships
with women were mainly physical, there existed towards his sister
a bond of affection which reveals another side of his character. He
had lost his father in awe-ful circumstances: he feared his dominant
mother; he cared for—rather than loved—Catherine, his Portuguese wife; he begat no lawful heirs. He felt towards his young sister, whom he called 'Minette' and saw so seldom, deep ties of family
love. Their relationship was fulfilled in a regular correspondence
which has more than a romantic appeal to the historian. It was the
device by which Charles II communicated privately with his brother-
in-law, Louis XIV. The letters were often sent by personal
messengers and so escaped the crude postal systems of the day
which denied regularity of delivery or privacy of contents.
Both Charles and Madame realized their importance for diplomatic
relations between England and France. In reaching an understanding
with France, there was no one 'so proper to make it as yourself',
he told Madame. 'If I do understand his or my own interests and
designs, a very fast friendship is good and necessary for us both,'
he said on another occasion, with reference to Louis XIV.

Yet there were factors which weakened the prospect. Firstly,
England as a whole was anti-French—an attitude clearly illustrated
by the incident of ambassadorial precedence in 1661, Secondly,
throughout the period 1660–67 Anglo-French relations were en-
tangled by the old problem of the sovereignty of the seas. Charles
II, in a letter to his sister, would not 'believe that any body who
desires my friendship' would refuse to salute English ships in the
Narrow Seas. Unfortunately Louis XIV required his own ships to
exact a salute from English ones and informed his ambassador,
Count D'Estrades, that he did not 'look for any accommodation

in the affair of the salute at sea' and regarded it as 'a point of honour connected with the fame of my crown'.

Neither side gave way, and some compromise was found in fleets avoiding each other, or saluting simultaneously. The issue was never taken to the point of conflict and its main importance is in illustrating Charles's loyalty to his navy.

Thirdly the two ambassadors who might have hastened an alliance were dilatory. Lord Holles resented Madame's role in diplomacy, while the Comte de Cominges could not speak English. Of Cominges, Charles wrote to Madame, 'I do not think (he) is very forward in the business. He finds upon all occasions so many difficulties.' Only when Louis XIV appointed the Marquis de Ruvigny as an extra envoy in 1664 did there seem a better prospect of success.

Fourthly, the imminent approach of war between England and Holland firmly prevented an alliance, in that the French were bound by a treaty of 1662 to help the Dutch. Louis's part in the second Anglo-Dutch war, which broke out in 1665, was brief in the extreme and confined to a few months, although a formal state of war between England and France existed from February 1666. To Ruvigny he wrote that it was a 'war on paper'. Charles and Madame stopped corresponding for some months, and a settlement of Anglo-French relations awaited the general ending of the Dutch war.

The fourth country to play a significant part in Restoration foreign policy was Portugal. Charles II had not made a marriage with a Spanish, Dutch or French girl. As for others, he had said: 'I hate Germans or princesses of cold countries. They are dull and foggy.' This ruled out eligible Protestant maidens in the Baltic. There remained Portugal. She was England's oldest ally, had helped Charles I with arms and munitions—a rare gesture in the Civil War—and had harboured Prince Rupert. In the end Cromwell had made the pace too hot and Portugal had succumbed, but the historic friendship was not broken. By the summer of 1660 the Portuguese ambassador in London, Francisco de Mello, later the Marquis de Sande, was ready to enter the English marriage lists on behalf of Catherine. She was the sister of Alfonso VI, the daughter of John IV and Luisa de Guzman and the granddaughter (through her mother) of the Duke of Medina Sidonia, of Armada fame. The ambassador had indeed first made approaches to General Monk some time earlier. He now faced, as we have seen, competition both from Spain and France. By the autumn—when Charles had personally rejected Mazarin's niece—the chances were good, despite the in-fighting of English politicians. Clarendon noted for example those (among whom was the persistent Henrietta Maria) who hoped to bestow 'some French lady upon the Queen, which would have better complied with other ends'. There were also plans to send the Earl of Bristol[1] to see some Italian ladies, the Earl trying to extract from Charles 'a promise not to proceed further in treaty with Portugal till his return'. Charles would have none of this, which he rightly interpreted as Spanish manoeuvring behind his back. Monk hoped a Portuguese marriage would ensure a continued anti-Spanish foreign policy.

Portugal had much to offer. The gift of Tangier and Bombay would provide bases for English Mediterranean and East Indian trade. An entrée to Portuguese colonial territories was assured. These—added to the possession of Jamaica—would furnish focal points for a world-wide trading economy. Finally there was a dowry of £500,000.

The turning-point in negotiations was Louis XIV's assurance to Clarendon that he welcomed the marriage: 'the king of France doth not only like the alliance, but on the contrary will, if it be needed assist the king of England with all his power, so that it be done in a secret way'. By the peace of the Pyrenees, France could not assist Portugal directly in her struggle with Spain. By encouraging an English marriage alliance, she could bring about English assistance against Spain.

Charles received unanimous support from his English council, who resented Spanish arrogance in the matter. By the summer of 1661 a contract was signed and the terms of the marriage treaty had been agreed upon. The treaty is a revealing document, indicating by its clauses how important the alliance was for Portugal. In return for Tangier, Bombay, the dowry, the infanta Catherine her-

---

[1] Son of the man who had negotiated with Spain in James I's reign.

self, and various trading concessions in Brazil and the Portuguese eastern empire,[1] the king of England was required to 'take the interest of Portugal and all its dominions to heart, defending the same with his utmost power by sea and land even as England itself'. If the king of Portugal were threatened by his enemies 'in any extraordinary power', the king of England was to dispatch all the ships he had in the Mediterranean and at Tangier to Portugal's 'succour and relief'. Nor could Charles make any agreement with Spain which might put Portuguese defences at risk—and this included returning Dunkirk or Jamaica to Spain. Finally a secret clause required Charles to help the Portuguese against the challenge of Dutch commerce.

So determined were the Portuguese to have the treaty that they declared anyone a heretic who objected to the marriage of the infanta with a Protestant king. National defence triumphed over religious antipathy. But the English were trusting no one. Tangier was taken over before a fleet sailed to collect Catherine.

England's new queen arrived and married Charles in May 1662. Pepys noted general approval; 'all the bells of the town rung, and bonfires made'. He also observed, more caustically, that despite the dowry the Portuguese had brought little actual cash with them.

How far did Charles II fulfil the marriage contract? The Spanish menace to Portugal was very real. Within a month of the marriage Spanish and Dutch ships were threatening Lisbon. Louis XIV, who had encouraged Charles in his Portuguese policy, reminded him that his honour was at stake. Charles despatched 'ten good ships of war'—exactly the number required of him in article xvi of the marriage treaty—and three thousand troops. A year later Clarendon complained to the ambassador in Lisbon that England lacked the 'money to send fleets or troops upon adventures'. The burden of a war in Portugal could not be 'sustained upon the weak shoulders of the Crown of England'. Nevertheless the troops fighting in Portugal —largely Cromwellian veterans—defeated the army of Don John of Austria, the Spanish commander, at the battle of Amegial (June

[1] Not much of which survived by 1661. By 1658 for example the last Portuguese had been expelled from Ceylon. The Dutch by this time had more East Indian territory than Portugal had ever held.

1663). It proved to be the last distinguished performance of English troops and their commanders in the seventeenth century.[1] It was enough, combined with the events of the peace of Aix-la-chapelle in 1668, to secure Portuguese independence from Spain.

Charles may be said to have met his obligations to Portugal. But what was the Portuguese alliance worth to England? Not much: by helping Portugal Charles was contributing to the decline of Spain. Though that would have been happening without any help from Charles, he was identified with it, and consequently with the rise of France. Even contemporaries realized in the 1660s that Spain was of less account than she had been in any man's memory. Such material gains as Tangier were soon discounted. Parliament was always reluctant to maintain it. In the end it was blown up: 'it had been better to have been done the first hour it was taken in dower from the Portuguese'. And the queen failed to give England an heir.

FINANCIAL NEEDS

It had been the financial lure of Catherine's dowry which had principally attracted Charles. The sum which she brought with her was almost equalled by that which he got for the sale of Dunkirk.

At the Restoration there were those who valued Cromwell's acquisition of Dunkirk. It was to Sir William Lockhart, its governor,[2] 'an excellent outworke for the defence of England' and a 'sally-port' for sallying forth against one's enemies. Lockhart spent money and labour in repairing and strengthening it. Charles replaced Lockhart by Sir Edward Harley,[3] who continued the reconstruction programme. But Harley's own replacement by Andrew Rutherford in May 1661 marked the appointment of a man, Charles wrote, who 'would know better how to live with his neighbours'. Charles later gave him the Governorship of Tangier. Rutherford got on well with the French, to whom Charles had decided to sell the harbour. There were indeed good reasons for such a sale.

---

[1] The Portuguese, largely on their own, defeated the Spanish at Villaviciosa in 1665. The news hastened Philip IV's death.

[2] And still the ambassador to France.

[3] Father of the politician of Queen Anne's reign.

It was difficult to defend, expensive to garrison, and unsuitable for trade. It represented a foreign policy which committed the English to a direct intervention in European affairs, and was in the Cromwellian rather than the Stuart tradition.

By article xvii of the marriage treaty Charles was forbidden to sell it back to Spain. It went on offer to France. For Louis XIV the purchase of Dunkirk represented an offset to Spanish influence in the Netherlands. It also provided a way of helping Portugal indirectly, by giving Charles the money to finance his forces there. As we have seen Louis was restricted by treaty from helping Portugal directly. Furthermore the sale began the process of making Charles II dependent on the French king. Clarendon realized how much Louis wanted Dunkirk and was able to secure a far higher price than the French originally proposed. Despite difficulties right up to the last, including bargaining as to whether the sum should be by instalments and as to who should be the trustees, Dunkirk was formally sold to the French in November 1662, though Charles never got more than three-quarters of the sale price of £400,000. Charles had run counter to traditional foreign policy by strengthening French interests and by the voluntary alienation of a British possession. Five thousand lives had been lost in securing Dunkirk: if the futility of loss of life is always true in war, this seems an example more glaring than most. In the years that followed Dunkirk might have been valuable.

The French certainly made good use of it, Vauban developing its forts, harbours and canals. Equal use might have been made of it by the English in the later conflicts of the seventeenth and eighteenth centuries. An MP said in the House of Commons in 1678: 'We shall never be quiet till Dunkirk be out of (French) hands; in the very mouth of the Thames, a new Algiers set up in Christendom; the midway betwixt your great rendezvous, northwards and westwards, of all your navigation.' Dunkirk as a base for piracy and privateering was an acquisition for England's rivals.

Charles II was under no obligation to maintain Cromwellian objectives in foreign policy, and the capture of Dunkirk had certainly been linked to the Protector's ambitions for Protestantism in Europe. The king's decision offended one Protestant head of state,

Frederick William the elector of Brandenburg, whose ambassador in London accused England of disassociation from the collective interests of continental Protestantism.

Charles II made short-term gains by the sale of Dunkirk. But its long-term significance was less assured. Dunkirk in French hands was viewed with suspicion at home. It was a factor in the fall of Charles's elder statesman, Clarendon. It invites one question, to which we must turn: what was the extent of Charles II's financial predicament?

At the Restoration heavy debts existed in public finance. They have been estimated at £3,000,000, arising from the military and naval commitments of the Commonwealth, the unsettled accounts of Charles I, and the expenses in exile of Charles II. It was accepted in 1660 that Charles II could not hope 'to live of his own', and a decaying medieval principle was at last abandoned. Instead parliament proposed that the king should have £1,200,000 a year, to be raised principally from customs and excise efficiently administered. There was also to be a Hearth Tax, expected to bring in £300,000 a year. This income was probably adequate in peacetime.

When Charles addressed parliament in 1660, he thanked them for sending him money to equip himself to come to England; 'the truth is I have lived principally ever since upon what I brought with me, which was indeed your money, for you sent it to me, and I thank you for it'. He apologized for not being able to give his guests a good meal when they came to see him. He was then voted his first £1,200,000.

Why then was Charles himself impoverished throughout his reign? There are several reasons. Most important was the fact that the proposed annual income was not forthcoming for fifteen years. The Hearth Tax in its first year, for instance, produced less than a third of the estimated yield. Secondly, the crown had to spend money on the army and navy beyond the calls of peacetime security. Thirdly, peculant officials regarded a share of the monies that passed through their hands as normal income for themselves. Charles got off to a bad start and never recovered. In his first year for example his expenditure was £470,000 greater than his income.

It is as reasonable for us to ask, as it was for his parliaments to contemplate, how he spent his income. From 1648 onwards he had been embroiled with mistresses and their offspring. By 1667 five of them had presented him with a total of nine illegitimate children. Their maintenance was a financial burden on Charles, especially when he ennobled them and their sons. It is probably true that Charles's mistresses did not influence his policies, but they did lighten his purse.

And his generosity went in other directions as well. To the disbanded Cromwellian army of forty thousand men he gave a week's extra pay. To many of those who had served him loyally in exile or who had helped him when a fugitive in England he gave presents. Indeed such people benefited more than royalists who had lost their estates. To those from whom Charles I had borrowed, Charles II paid sums throughout his reign. When the Fire of London burnt down the Customs House, Charles gave £10,000 for the building of another. But none of these outlays approximated to the general excess of expenditure over revenue. Charles lived with his accumulating debts from year to year. Generous as he was, the extent of his poverty can be gauged from the fact that he even held on to £10,000 which a parliamentary delegation had intended for his loved sister Henriette-Anne just before her marriage. He wrote to her in 1662; 'nothing but pure necessity and impossibility hath kept me hitherto from paying what I owe you'—an allusion either to the debt or her dowry, or both.

Ironically one of the worst burdens upon Charles was the war with the Dutch. The nation showed much more enthusiasm than he for it, and parliament voted £5,500,000 towards its cost, which still left Charles with heavy war expenses to pay for. Thus in the first seven years of the reign the stage was set for that dependency on France for revenue which the sale of Dunkirk and even the Portuguese marriage had foreshadowed.

So desperate indeed had he been for the Dunkirk money that he obtained a capital sum greater than Louis' initial payment by going to a French banker who quoted him 16 per cent interest. Charles accepted the hard bargain and forty-six cart-loads of silver soon made their way to England, to pay for army and navy arrears, royal jewellery, and to be minted into coinage.

H

Financially therefore Charles was in no position to make much contribution to the second of the three Anglo-Dutch wars of the seventeenth century, which broke out in March 1665. From the Restoration onwards, war was always a predictable event since there were those in both nations who wished it. Commercial factors far more than political ones were the cause.

Commercially disputes occurred wherever English and Dutch met in colonial places and in home waters. In the East Indies the two trading companies clashed over the seizure of English ships, the possession of the Moluccan island of Poele-rum and the English acquisition of Bombay—though this was a matter of Dutch jealousy rather than a challenge to trade. Certainly by 1660 Dutch ascendency over all comers in the East Indies was assured.

In North America the English acquisition of New Amsterdam in September 1664 struck a blow at Dutch colonial settlements in the New Netherland—between New England and Virginia. Charles II laconically wrote to Madame; 'You will have heard of our taking of New Amsterdam. 'Tis a place of great importance to trade. It did belong to England heretofore, but the Dutch by degrees drove our people out and built a very great town, but we have got the better of it, and 'tis now called New York.'

The acquisition of New Amsterdam may be linked to the attack on Dutch interests on the Guinea coast of Africa in the same year. The English obtained gold and seized the island of Goree, only to lose it again in December to the Dutch admiral De Ruyter. Both the American and African enterprises had behind them the authority of James, Duke of York.

Rivalry and prestige at sea found expression in English claims to sovereignty in the narrow seas, continued disputes over fisheries, and requests for compensation to English sailors for losses through attacks.

English commercial hostility at home was shown in the passing of the 1660 Navigation Act and in increased investment in joint-stock enterprises. The object of such measures was to stimulate the economy at the expense of the Dutch, against whom the 1660 Act was intended to be far more effective than that of 1651.

The political aspects of Anglo-Dutch relations were of less significance, but cannot be ignored. We have seen that an Anglo-Dutch marriage alliance came to nothing. In 1662 the two countries renewed the agreements made in the treaty of Westminster in 1654, but left untouched the major issues of discord. Clarendon told Sir George Downing, the ambassador at The Hague, to avoid matters which would 'raise present dispute, and which may be taken up whenever we think fit to do so'. The year 1662 in England was no time for further troubles; the Anglican settlement was being established, and Clarendon informed Downing that a settlement with the Dutch republic might pacify English republican elements. It also allowed time for the economy to recover and the navy to be strengthened.

At the same time the Dutch had made their treaty with France, which bound Louis XIV to help the Dutch in the event of war. It was the nagging doubt as to how energetically France would aid the Dutch which made English moderates hesitate to fight. The treaty was certainly a diplomatic triumph for the Dutch leader, John de Witt, in that he appeared to have secured a strong ally in the event of English hostility.

For Charles II there was a personal political aspect. Cromwellian policy, as we saw earlier, had excluded the Orange family from the Dutch stadtholdership. Charles, when he sailed from The Hague in 1660, had indicated his concern for William II's widow, Mary; 'the princess, my sister, and the Prince of Orange, my nephew, persons who are extremely dear to me'. The Dutch States-General had undertaken to maintain and educate William, but promised no more. When William's mother died of smallpox in January 1661 Charles became his guardian, declaring that now his 'honour required him' to undo Cromwell's policy of exclusion.

This proved a first flush of enthusiasm on his assuming responsibility for the boy. During the next three years Charles was on the side of caution. While he hoped the nation would be ready for war, he did not propose to rush into it. To Madame he wrote in June 1664—the first time he mentioned the possibility of war to her —'The States keep a great bragging and noise, but I believe when it comes to it, they will look twice before they leap. I never saw so great an appetite to a war as is in both this town and country, especially in the parliament men, who I am confident would pawn their estates to maintain a war, but all this shall not govern me, for I will look merely to what is just and best for the honour and good of England.'

Charles, with all his faults, placed the honour of England high in his affections and loyalties. The fondness he had acquired for it in exile never left him. He was not ready to prosceute the war on the personal issue of the Dutch Exclusion. In this he was unlike his father and grandfather, who had made the personal affair of the Palatinate so much a matter of national politics.

Nor was it in Charles's financial interest to fight a war. However generous and impulsive the Commons might prove to be—and they voted £2,500,000 in 1664—he knew that the net result would probably be to increase his own debts. Finally he valued the growing relationship with France, 'more considerable than that of the Hollanders' and was reluctant to see it jeopardized. Here again it was a personal rather than a national view.

It would be an exaggeration to say that Charles's foreign policy at this stage was—in the tradition of James I—thoroughly out of tune with that of the country at large, but it would be fair to recognize that there was a difference in tempo. Someone who agreed with Charles more than most was Sir George Downing, who felt that political weaknesses in Holland would work against Dutch prospects in war.

Indeed, as in 1652, it was the English who were more determined to fight than the Dutch. Charles's meeting with the Dutch ambassadors as late as June 1664 left him with the impression that when it came to the point their nation was not prepared for war. They asked him not to let ships which he was preparing to send to sea 'go out, lest by the indiscretion of some of the captains the quarrel might begin'. To Madame he commented, 'You may guess by such a simple proposition whether these people are not afraid'. Charles's letters to Madame were never pure politics; this one ended: 'I am just now called away by very good company to sup upon the water, so I can say no more.'

Nevertheless by the spring of 1665 extremists on both sides brought about the second Anglo-Dutch War. John De Witt, though not an extremist himself, was convinced that his navy was able to fight successfully. In England commercial and political advocates of war successfully joined forces. They included unemployed Cromwellian soldiers and sailors—men like George Monk, now Duke of Albemarle, and William Penn. There were also the enemies of Lord Clarendon, who saw a war as a means of destroying his influence. City men with money in the Royal African Company and the East and West India Company had vested interests in war. Even Charles himself might not be the loser if trade expanded and more customs revenues came his way. On 4 March, as Pepys noted, 'this day was proclaimed at the 'Change the war with Holland'.

THE SECOND DUTCH WAR

By comparison with the wars of the twentieth century, or indeed the world-wide conflicts of the eighteenth, the second Anglo-Dutch War was a minor affair. The two sides between them lost under fifty ships and less than 10,000 men. There were two summer campaigns in 1665 and 1666, together with some military activity in the winter of 1665–6 and a disastrous two days for the English in June 1667.

Victory was evenly distributed. The opening battle at Lowestoft in June 1665 brought English rejoicing and Dutch recriminations. Pepys delighted in going to the Dolphin Tavern 'where all we officers of the navy met with the Commissioners of the Ordnance by agreement, and dined'. The Dutch second-in-command, Jan Evertsen, was court-martialled.

Two years later to the month it was the turn of the Dutch. They stole up the Thames, sailed up the Medway, broke the boom at Gillingham, and took as prize the *Royal Charles*, the very flagship which had brought Charles II from their own shores to England.[1] Now praise and blame took different courses. 'The brave heroes of our fatherland manfully forwarded this great work,' recorded a Dutch observer. Thomas Povey[2] told Pepys that

[1] Its stern can still be seen in the Maritime Museum at Amsterdam.
[2] Povey had not yet received the favours from court he expected. Pepys knew him well, and found him a useful source of information and gossip.

it was 'out of possibility for us to escape undone: a lazy prince, no Council, no money, no reputation at home or abroad'.

These were the first and last encounters. In between there had been an English attempt in 1665 to capture an East India merchant-fleet sheltering in Bergen in Norway, and a major Four-Day battle in 1666 in the Thames, when Albemarle met Admiral de Ruyter. The battle was a clear-cut victory to neither side.

In January 1666 the French had entered the war because of their treaty arrangements with the Dutch. They never fought at sea, although the fear of their fleet led to Prince Rupert detaching himself in the Four-Day battle to keep an eye on them. French troops were involved however in a campaign in the winter of 1665–6, which may be briefly mentioned as an illustration of the intricacies of seventeenth-century foreign policy. Charles II had secured the services of the warrior-bishop of Munster, Bernard von Galen. With sixteen thousand men and four thousand horse the bishop attacked the Dutch on their landward flank. Prince Maurice of Nassau left his governorship of Cleves to command a hastily-raised Dutch army, and Brunswick and French forces joined in. The threat of Brandenburg attacking him also led the bishop to sue for peace. The episode had cost Charles II £250,000—money he could ill-afford.

This affair apart, it was a war fought at sea. Both sides had been better prepared than in 1652, with de Witt and the Duke of York equally assiduous in supervising the work of their dockyards. If the English had more ships and larger ones, the Dutch had more guns and more men. Fire-ships played a large part in battle. It was a war during which the tactics of line-formation made considerable advance. A Dutch critic noticed how the English 'stayed on a tack for half an hour until they put themselves into the order in which they meant to fight'. The techniques of Nelson's day were being developed.

Domestic affairs severely crippled English morale. Pepys' elation at the victory in June 1665 was modified by another entry: 'This day I did see two or three houses marked with a red cross upon the doors, which was a sad sight to me.' The Plague had come to London. Fifteen months later came the Fire. Charles, who had avoided the worst of the Plague by visiting, in a mood of escapism, the west country lanes through which he had once ridden to safety, was a hero during the Fire. A contemporary declared that what survived at all of London was thanks to Charles's personal bravery and organization. But Plague and Fire had taken a collective toll of lives, property and money. Insurance was in its infancy and no one reaped any compensation. During the winter of 1666–7 confidence fell, prices rose, sailors mutinied, citizens froze,[1] rumours flourished[2] and republicans stirred. The government, financially paralysed, decided on no naval campaign for 1667—hence the disaster in the Medway—and opened negotiations for peace.

The Medway incident hastened the peace settlement, the treaty of Breda. In itself it was not a document of striking significance. Both England and Holland agreed to keep the possessions that each had held before the war, and those they acquired during it. Thus the Dutch retained Poele-Rum, while England secured her war-gains of New York, New Jersey and Delaware. These American settlements gave the English control of the eastern seaboard of the continent and linked the colonies in the tropical south with those in the temperate north, besides giving the English the command of New York for just under a century. But contemporaries did not attach great importance to these gains. Some concessions were made in the English Navigation Act and the English agreed to a more limited area in which they would expect their ships to be saluted. The settlement restored the balance of power, as between the two nations, to the Dutch and went some way towards moderating the bitterness in their relations. The elements of conflict—and a third war—remained. Supporters of appeasement of the Dutch were not fashionable. Nevertheless the years of worst antagonism now lay in the past.

Although de Witt had strengthened his personal position in the Netherlands, the real victor was Louis XIV. His intervention in 1666 had been partly due to his treaty commitments to the Dutch and partly to his hopes of the Spanish succession, strengthened by

---

[1] Coal was £30 a cauldron, and the Thames froze over.
[2] For example, that the Fire had been caused by Catholics.

the death of his father-in-law Philip IV in 1665. If the Dutch had suspected his ambitions on the Spanish Netherlands, they might have made a separate peace with England to defend the Flanders coastline. For a start he sought in the Law of Devolution to acquire a large part of the southern Netherlands. In May 1667 his troops were capturing forts and overrunning the Spanish Netherlands before Breda was even signed. The success of his armies frightened both Dutch and English, whose war had been to Louis' advantage. How Charles—and England—reacted to this threat after 1667 will be the subject of the next chapter. Meanwhile, the English king faced a crisis in government which was of significance for his future foreign policy.

At the Restoration Charles's principal advisers on foreign affairs had been Edward Hyde, Earl of Clarendon—whom he had appointed Lord Chancellor in 1658—Thomas Wriothesley, Earl of Southampton, James Butler, Duke of Ormonde, and George Monk, Duke of Albemarle. All except Monk had been loyalists throughout. Monk had worked his passage in the weeks before the Restoration.[1] The youngest, Ormonde, was fifty. Clarendon himself recorded that they worked well together, in a 'united concurrence of judgements and affections'. The tradition and stability they represented were important to Charles at the outset.

Of these men Clarendon was unquestionably the most important. He stood for strong executive government, exclusive Anglicanism and a pacific foreign policy, since he felt this would make it easier for Charles to bring 'his own dominions into that temper of obedience, they ought to be in'. But events were greater than the man, and Clarendon was the ironic witness of the war against the Dutch, and associated with its failure. The nation demanded a sacrifice and so did the politicians.

By 1667 younger men such as Henry Bennet, Lord Arlington and Anthony Ashley Cooper, Earl of Shaftesbury, were crowding in on Clarendon, wishing he would go. But the real challenge came from the legislature, the lower house of which was Charles II's

---

[1] Ormonde's peerage as an Irish earldom, went back to 1328. Southampton's peerage was a Tudor creation. All the others mentioned on this page were ennobled by Charles II. See p. 164.

'Cavalier' Parliament, which he was destined to have until 1679. When Charles II first met the members, he spoke with all the diplomacy and something of the artistry of language of Queen Elizabeth: 'there are few of you of whom I have not heard so much good that I am as sure as I can be of anything that is to come that you will concur with me, and that I shall concur with you, in all things which may advance the peace, plenty and prosperity of the nation. I shall be exceedingly displeased else.' The mood did not last. The house quickly showed a religious intolerance foreign to Charles's nature, it was unenthusiastic over revenue, and as the years went by it became more and more filled with men with whom Charles found himself less in sympathy. Nor did Charles ensure that the ministers closest to him sat in the Commons. In this he made the same mistake as his grandfather. Men like Arlington were ennobled by Charles and lost to the Commons.

Clarendon's closeness to the crown offended the Commons. Pepys tells us that he had dismissed them contemptuously as 'country gentlemen only fit to give money'. There was an attempt to impeach him, resisted by the House of Lords. In the end the fallen minister took matters into his own hands and fled to France. Charles recorded that so long as Clarendon continued in office it was 'impossible to do those things with the parliament that must be done' or the government lost.

Charles no longer needed an avuncular figure, and disliked the strictures of a moralist. Clarendon found little sympathy from an impoverished country ill-suited to sustain the prosperous new mansion he was building for himself. His day was done. Charles turned to other men, and to policies which would have made little appeal to the fallen chancellor.

9   The French alignment, 1667–74

Lord! what miseries are mortal men subject to, and what confusion and mischief do the avarice, anger and ambition of Princes cause in the world!

John Evelyn

THE CABAL
Emotion played no part in Charles II's choice of men. No Robert Carr or George Villiers found rapid elevation to earldoms or dukedoms. Ladies like Barbara Palmer and Louise de Kéroualle were more successful in becoming duchesses. Nor was sincerity of purpose and respectability of demeanour necessarily the path to office. There is no one to match in character Cromwell's Whitelocke. A combination of wit, talent, astuteness, opportunities and a careless approach to morals both public and private might describe the collective qualities of the men who replaced Clarendon. But it would be extremely unjust to ascribe all these characteristics to any one individual.

Clarendon's successors provided Charles with five men who were closest to him in government from 1667 to 1674.[1] Other men were consulted from time to time, notably Lord Arundell, but these five were the signatories of a public treaty in December 1670. Only two of them signed its secret counterpart six months earlier. They were quickly nicknamed a Cabal, from the initials of their names. Under that nickname we may briefly comment upon their careers, before seeing what part they played in the central event of Charles's foreign policy—his political liaison with Louis XIV.

Sir Thomas Clifford served as a young member in the Restoration parliament. His abilities were noticed by Arlington and he went on

[1] One of them, Clifford, died at the end of 1673.

a diplomatic mission to Denmark. He was present at a key meeting[1] with Charles II in January 1669 and throughout the next eighteen months played an important part in the negotiations with France, often acting as the draftsman of Charles's propositions. Of all the Cabal, he was the most strongly sympathetic towards the Catholic faith. Alone amongst them Clifford sat in the House of Commons, where he had his uses as a parliamentary manager on behalf of Charles's interests. Like his father and grandfather before him, Charles took insufficient care to leave men close to him in the Commons. Only in the closing months of his life did Clifford spoil a career of conspicuous loyalty to the crown by currying the favour of the hostile Commons of 1673. He was seen to be drinking with those who drank, declaiming with those of a serious frame of mind, and worshipping according to the Anglican rites with the pious. But he faced the Test Act with sincerity, and died soon afterwards reconciled to the Catholic fold.

Arlington, formerly Sir Henry Bennet, was a member of the Cavalier parliament whom Charles raised to the peerage in 1665 and elevated to an earldom in 1672. Of the eleven men who held the office of secretary of state[2] in Charles's reign, Arlington's tenure was by far the longest. He was appointed in 1662 and fell in the reshuffle of 1674. Even afterwards Charles turned to him, despite the suspicions of the Commons concerning such an undoubted 'king's man'. Indeed, he wore his loyalty on his nose—a black patch covered a scar won in the Civil War. Loyalty, together with efficiency, linguistic ability and the knack of interpreting Charles's whims—both political and personal—explain his survival. Caroline politicians in the 1670s did not need to worry about their heads, unlike their counterparts under Henry a century or more earlier. But cliques could break them, and even get them sent to the Tower of London for a spell. Arlington's own grandfather, Sir John Bennet, never more than a back-bench MP in Elizabeth's and James's reign, had been fined and imprisoned at the end of his days. Arlington himself eventually faced possible impeachment in 1674, but the Commons let him alone. He defended his part in Charles's

---

[1] See below, p. 122.

[2] There were always two secretaries of state at a time in the seventeenth century.

French policies by saying that he had shared in collective decisions—
'my opinion was concurrent'. He denied he had aspirations to be a
'prime minister of state', of which Sir Charles Wheeler[1] accused him,
and his general civility saved him. Prime minister or not, no man
stood closer to Charles II after the fall of Clarendon.

Buckingham (George Villiers, the second duke) sat in the Lords
from the moment of his majority. He was a privy councillor, but
never held a major political office. He had loyally served the Stuarts,
twice seeing his estates confiscated and then restored. Charles and he
had known each other all their lives, had fought together at
Worcester and kept in touch in exile. Buckingham was politically
active throughout the 1660s. Men feared his tongue and Charles
himself held the arrogant duke in some awe. He had little sympathy
with the Anglicanism of Charles's Commons, and favoured a general
policy of religious toleration. He was not sufficiently reliable and
certainly not pro-Catholic enough to be in on the secret Dover
negotiations, but was sent by Charles in the autumn of 1670 to
negotiate with Louis XIV a public treaty. After the challenge by
the Commons to the king's executive in 1674 Buckingham fell from
influence. He behaved with little dignity before the Commons,
saddling Arlington with all the blame for the French alliance.[2] But
to the end of his life he fought for the principle of toleration, and
this is to his credit.

Ashley, who as Sir Anthony Ashley Cooper was raised to the
peerage in 1661, and advanced to the Earldom of Shaftesbury in
1672, did not have the strong undeviating associations of Arlington
or Buckingham. Although he had raised a regiment at his own
expense to fight for Charles I, he had later commanded parliamentary
forces. He then served in Cromwell's Council of State, but took
part in negotiations with Charles II in March 1660. Shortly after the
Restoration he was pardoned for his associations with the Protect-

[1] Sir Charles Wheeler was a back-bench MP watchful of the Commons interests and in a time of much corruption concerned with the proper use of public
money.
[2] In retrospect, not an unreasonable attitude. But neither Buckingham nor the
House of Commons knew in 1674 of Arlington's real role in the Dover negotiations.

orate, ennobled and made chancellor of the exchequer.[1] He was not
privy to the secret negotiations leading to the treaty of Dover, for
three reasons: he had shown himself more interested in colonial
trading ventures than European politics; he was 'presbyterian' in
sympathy and his views on toleration had dissenters rather than
catholics in mind; his vacillating loyalties in the past made his trust
unreliable to Charles. Until he was asked to participate in the
arrangements leading to the public treaty he was only on the
perimeter of great events. In 1672 Charles made him lord chancellor,
but he fell a year later when the Commons attacked him for issuing
writs for parliamentary elections. After a discreet interval of
retirement, he returned to politics—alone amongst the Cabal—to
play a major part in the events of the following ten years.

Lauderdale (John Maitland, the first duke), who succeeded his
father to the earldom in the Scottish peerage in 1645, was yet another
of the Cabal who had been associated with Charles in earlier days,
serving with him at Worcester. He was a prisoner-of-war for nine
years after the battle and must have welcomed the Restoration with
more than ordinary enthusiasm. He came of strong Scottish ante-
cedents—a great uncle was the Maitland of Lethington who served
Mary Queen of Scots.

Lauderdale's career was spent in his own country, where he
enforced episcopacy again, despite his personal presbyterian sympathies. He was a dominant figure in Scotland, a 'man very national,
and truly the honour of our nation for wits and parts'. He was
supremely loyal to Charles, determining—as he wrote to the king—
that 'the whole course of my life shall be to obey you in your own
way'. His authority in Scotland was severe, though it is arguable
that the country in the 1660s and 1670s needed such a man because
of its religious discords and political dissensions. He had a Scotsman's
love of learning, though his knowledge of the classics and of Hebrew
faded in the business of politics after 1660. That business was
essentially Scottish, and he saw his rôle as enforcing the power of
the crown and acting with some independence as Scottish secretary
of state. There were no reasons at all why he should have been aware

---

[1] Not then a great office of state.

of the secret negotiations leading to the treaty of June 1670, though his status in Charles's ministry entitled him to take part in the simulated events of the autumn of that year. Lauderdale was attacked by the Commons in 1673 with more vigour than were any of his colleagues, simply because there was no clique to whom he could turn for support. Not until 1707 were there Scottish members at Westminster. But if he had no recognizable Scottish friends, he had plenty of Scottish enemies—men like the Duke of Hamilton and the Earl[1] of Tweeddale who rushed to London to tell tales of his private monopolies, his sale of offices, his corruption of the mint. But these mattered less to the Commons than Lauderdale's own report that he could march 20,000 Scotsmen to the king's service in England. This was enough to finish him in their eyes, but Charles still retained him in his Scottish service until 1680.

Such were the men closest to Charles after the fall of Clarendon. As a Cabal their unity was a loose one, but sufficient to bring out a tract called *The Alarum* against them in 1669, declaring they used 'the king to shield them from the arrows of parliament'. Another contemporary tract, called *England's appeal from the private Cabal at Whitehall to the great council of the nation*, attacked them in 1673 for the French alliance.

THE TRIPLE ALLIANCE

In the closing months of 1667 both English and Dutch observers watched the course of events in the Spanish Netherlands with some alarm. De Witt feared the French advance through Flanders, Brabant and Hainault. Arlington was the English politician who took the most realistic view: at that point not only did he oppose French aggression, but also visualized a Franco-Dutch bargain over the Spanish Netherlands. He knew of de Witt's friendship towards France, which amounted to a policy of appeasement. De Witt was only ready to see France restrained if she were sufficiently satisfied with her gains at the expense of Spain. It was not a state of affairs which appealed to the English, who saw commercial and political threats in a Flanders coastline in hostile hands.

[1] Later Marquis of Tweeddale.

It was therefore in the English interest, rather more than in the Dutch, for an alliance to be formed between the two countries, whose rivalry had for so long been central to their relationship. By December 1667, after some weeks of diplomatic exchanges, the English government was determined on swift action. Indeed, it is the speed of events that gives them particular interest. On 1 January 1668, the committee for foreign affairs met Sir William Temple and gave him his instructions.

Temple was at the time envoy in Brussels. He was a man with only limited diplomatic experience, but well suited to represent English interests at The Hague. He was a good linguist, who had given considerable thought to the need for Anglo-Dutch co-operation. He had discussed it at the Breda peace negotiations in 1667, and in October of that year, after meeting de Witt, had written somewhat euphorically to Arlington that the choice lay between 'an easy peace' between the two countries or 'a glorious war' on their part against France. His letter crossed with a much cooler one from Arlington, doubting the long-term value of a balance between England and Holland on the one hand and the French on the other— a subject for 'witty men' to talk about out of doors. By Christmas Arlington was ready to give it a try.

Temple's time-table by seventeenth-century travelling standards was impressive. He had been recalled from Brussels at Christmas. He left England again on January 2nd in Charles's yacht. Travelling conditions in Holland were particularly difficult owing to frost, and he reached The Hague on the 7th, meeting de Witt late that night. On January 13th an agreement was reached and put on paper. By the 23rd the document had been to England and come back again ratified.[1] The agreement is known as the Triple Alliance of 1668, since Sweden shortly afterwards associated herself with the Dutch and the English. Three questions arise. What decisions were taken in such haste? Were they important? Did they last?

The major decisions of the alliance were twofold. Firstly, the English and the Dutch agreed in detailed terms to help each other if invaded. Secondly, the treaty spelt out the concessions which Spain

---

[1] By comparison, the Anglo-Spanish commercial treaty of May 1667 came after nine months of discussion. It was not ratified for a further four.

should make to France and proposed a frontier between the two
countries in the Netherlands.

Their importance can be exaggerated. France had already discussed the question of a temporary frontier with the United
Provinces, and had reached agreement upon the line defined in the
treaty. Furthermore, France had made a secret agreement with the
Habsburg Emperor Leopold I on 19 January 1668, which laid down
plans for the ultimate partition of the Spanish Empire, including of
course the Spanish Netherlands.

Charles II of Spain had come to the throne in 1665. It seemed
unlikely that this sad and diseased Habsburg would produce an heir.
Both Louis and Leopold awaited his death and his vacant Empire.
The Spanish Charles kept them waiting thirty-five years. But for
the moment Louis XIV had reached an understanding on the
question of Partition which from his point of view made the 'utmost
endeavours and industry' of England and Holland towards a Franco-
Spanish peace less important.

Three months after the treaty came the settlement between
France and Spain at Aix-la-Chapelle. It embodied the terms suggested in the Triple Alliance. Louis XIV restored Franche-Comté,
which he had over-run in the winter months, contrary to the
conventions of warfare. Spain ceded such places in Flanders as
Tournai, Oudenarde, Lille and Armentières. Their names have the
ring of battles in other and later wars. There is some significance in
this, for their cession to France produced no true peace. The Spanish
Netherlands, the Austrian Netherlands, Belgium—call them what
you will—remained scarred territory in a divided Europe for three
more centuries.[1] The Triple Alliance was probably a decisive factor
in bringing Louis XIV to the negotiating table. As such it had some
importance. Aix-la-Chapelle has been called by different historians
a 'humiliation' for Louis XIV and a 'diplomatic victory' for him.
Yet he was scarcely humiliated, nor was he diplomatically victorious.
He was invited to respect the strength of his neighbours and for the
moment he wisely did so. In January 1668 the Triple Alliance had

---

[1] These lines were written in the first week of January 1973; when Belgium, in
particular its capital of Brussels, seemed to be assuming a happier rôle, as a place
for leaders of a new nine-nation European Community to meet.

tried to provide a tactful settlement, neither offending Louis nor insulting Spain. To the German historian von Ranke, writing in the nineteenth century, its importance lay in its formulation of a peace in the best interests of the European community.[1] If that be the view to take of the Alliance, then it was a failure. For Louis XIV resented a coalition against him and was angered by the attitude of the Dutch. His revenge followed.

Events did not stand still, and we must pose the third question. Did the decisions of the Triple Alliance last?

As a trinity of nations, no. Sweden had participated for two reasons. Her diplomat at The Hague, Count Dohna, was hostile to France and sympathetic to England, with whom his country had enjoyed reasonable relations during the Commonwealth, strengthened by a commercial treaty in 1665. Furthermore, France had been markedly sympathetic to two of Sweden's rivals, Poland and Brandenburg, within the past eighteen months. But Sweden's association with the other two powers was much vaguer, despite the concluding sentence of the Swedish part of the document, which spoke of their relationship having the 'substance as well as the form of a triple agreement'. Sweden had specific interests which were not central to the western European scene. By 1668 Dohna was dead, and with him went the mainspring of Sweden's interest in the Triple Alliance. The Baltic soon claimed her attention again.

Secondly, the alliance did not last because Charles II, James, Duke of York, Arlington, Buckingham and Clifford were all pulling against it by the summer of 1668. All those who communicated with France, besides those who fostered Catholic interests, loosened the ties between England and Holland. As the next part of this chapter will show, the negotiations leading to the treaty of Dover, and the consequences of that treaty, neutralized the worth of the Triple Alliance.

Yet in another sense it did last. The secret clauses of the treaty had provided for action if Louis XIV refused to accept Spanish concessions. 'Then England and the United Provinces shall be bound

---

[1] One must consider Ranke's opinion in relation to his nationality, the time at which he was writing and hs own outlook as an historian. In translation, he used the word 'community' (see the footnote on page 120).

I

and obliged with all their united force and power to make war against France and to continue the war till things shall be restored to that condition in which they were at the time when peace was made upon the borders of both kingdoms in the Pyrenean mountains.' Here lay the declaration of English foreign policy against the aggression of Louis XIV and the commitment to policies which extended throughout the eighteenth century. But for the moment Arlington briefly rejoiced in the Triple Alliance, 'God be thanked it is done'; Pepys, more sombrely, felt 'safe for this year'; Charles II assured his sister he had done nothing prejudicial to France. De Witt gave a banquet and turned to domestic affairs.

Louis XIV sent Charles Colbert, Marquis de Croissy, brother of the French minister Jean-Baptiste Colbert, to England as his ambassador. His arrival in August 1668 ushers in a period of treaty-making whose slowness is in marked contrast to the swiftness of the Triple Alliance negotiations.

TOWARDS DOVER

From June 1668 to June 1670 a series of events took place concerning which we can establish facts and consider motives. It is a fact that Charles II declared his intention of becoming a Catholic to various people at different times. For example, he told his brother, Arlington, Arundell and Clifford on 25 January 1669 that he proposed to become a Catholic and sought advice 'about the ways and methods fittest to be taken for the settling of the Catholic religion in his kingdoms and to consider of the time most proper to declare himself'.[1] In a coded letter to Madame on 22 March 1669 he spoke of his intentions towards the Catholic religion.

It is also a fact that he was determined on a French alliance. In a letter to Madame on 8 July 1668 he declared he had 'always' desired to 'make a stricter alliance with France than there has been hitherto'. Six months later, on 20 January 1669, he told her of his desire to 'enter into a personal friendship with (Louis XIV) and to unite our interests so for the future as there may never be any jealousies between us'. By March 1669, as his coded letter mentioned in the

---

[1] It is true there is only one source for this evidence, the Duke of York himself —a biased observer.

preceding paragraph suggests, he was deeply involved both in discussing his conversion and in proposing an alliance.

If these were the facts, what were Charles II's motives? Were they religious? Up to a point, the answer is yes. He had seen more of Catholic Europe than Protestant Europe. Living within four generations of the Reformation, he may have believed that western Christendom could unite in a restoration of Catholic authority. He must have recognized the parity in hierarchy between absolute king and Catholic kingdom. Catholics had helped him to escape after Worcester. Most of his surviving relations and two of his mistresses were Catholics. He died a Catholic.

Were his motives political? Here it can be argued that Charles believed in the virtue of an alliance with France rather than with the Dutch on four grounds; that the Dutch were the historic enemy of seventeenth-century Englishmen; that a Franco-English alliance, prevented a Franco-Dutch one; that such an alliance was in the best interests of the English navy; that he enjoyed a kinship with the French court which found no answering echo in the States-General or for that matter in Spain, Sweden or the Empire.

Were the motives financial? The total sum ultimately *offered* to Charles by Louis XIV in June 1670 was £350,000. He actually received £140,000. Since Charles always needed money it seems fair to accept this as a contributory factor. The expectations were high but the reality proved low.

Were they personal? In this sense one can argue that Charles desired to be rid of a dependence on parliament, which only financial freedom could bring him. It does not seem a wholly convincing view. Charles prorogued parliament with frequency throughout his reign and dispensed with its services altogether for the last four years. Yet its members were never the burden to his concept of kingship which they were to his father and grandfather. Charles was too human to accept fully the divinity of kingship—axiomatic for princes who aspired to absolutism.

Were Charles's motives imperial? In a very long letter Madame wrote to Charles on 21 September 1669, there is a revealing passage: 'It is true that by establishing your dominion on the ruins of that of Holland you will also contribute towards increasing that of the king (of France) who aspires not less than yourself to becoming supreme in commerce.' It was a view Charles did not reject in reply. It offered him absolutism in a different sense. The acquisition of commercial dominance and imperial power was more positive than a mere rejection of parliament. If it were to succeed, Charles would have vanquished the Dutch, matched Louis XIV, pleased the City, trimmed the parliamentarians to size, and usefully employed the navy. He could then ensure religious toleration for men and women who sought it. He would be a king not forgotten by posterity. Let this be a view to take of the complicated and tortuous diplomacy which occupied him in 1669 and 1670.

Having examined Charles's motives, we may ask what were Louis's? It would be wrong to stress too much a religious motive behind them. He was not especially concerned with the conversion of Charles or of England, and was anyway sceptical about the prospects of success. Despite what clause 9 of the secret treaty was to say, neither Charles nor Louis pushed the issue of Catholicism after June 1670. Fundamentally, Louis's motives were political. He sought a ruthless war against the Dutch in order that they would make no resistance to his ultimate intention of acquiring the Spanish Netherlands and Franche Comté. When he sent the Marquis de Croissy as ambassador to England in August 1668, he informed him he had been appointed to the most important diplomatic post in the king's service and instructed him to arrange an alliance with England—and break off the Triple Alliance. Charles told Madame he was 'satisfied with' de Croissy, and felt that his appointment showed the seriousness of Louis' intentions; he said that his own 'inclinations' were still the same, 'I hope in the end to bring all things to what I wish'.

The following summer (July 1669) Louis XIV wrote a personal letter to Charles II, carried by Arundell: 'I am sure you will acknowledge that it is with justice that you have expressed to me so obliging a desire to bind ourselves together in a stricter alliance, since I desire no less than you this new bond between our hearts and interests.'

In the last eighteen months before the signing of the treaty—from January 1669 to June 1670—participants in the enterprise were busy in a number of ways on both sides of the channel. There were

secret 'working-parties' in Paris and in London of which neither
the French nor English ambassadors to each other's countries were
at first aware. Louis, Charles, Madame, Arlington, Buckingham and
Clifford all engaged in correspondence and meetings with only a
limited awareness of each other's knowledge of events. A mathema-
tician could draw Venn diagrams to illustrate their interlocking
relationship.

There was Charles's continuing correspondence with Madame,
which from March 1669 was in cipher. At first the cipher was so
elementary that any schoolboy or schoolgirl could have solved it.
He told Madame that he was sending across *mpsebswoefmm*[1] as the
bearer of his proposals to Lord XIV. This person would not be
suspected as he was in the household of Queen Henrietta Maria.
Later the code became more sophisticated, in that people and places,
together with the vital words 'religion', 'catholic', 'parliament' and,
significantly, 'commerce', were given numbers. Three numbers
were allotted to each secret word, and separated by 26 in every
instance. Thus, Louis XIV was 100, 126 and 152, while Charles
himself was 334, 360 and 386. Twelve people in the two countries
were given numbers. It reminds us how few were involved in the
diplomacy leading to the secret treaty of Dover.

In the year 1669 Charles wrote to Madame about once a month.
An extract from one letter will illustrate the secrecy of negotiations,
their complexity, the extent to which Charles had involved himself,
and the varying information possessed by others. The letter, written
on 7 June 1669, is given in its original coding.[2] It indicates how
secret was the whole affair, culminating indeed in a document which
was not formally revealed to the world until one hundred and sixty
years later.

'Upon the whole matter I see no kind of necessity of telling 112
of the secret now, nor indeed till 270 is in a better readiness to make
use of 297 towards the great business. It will be enough that 164 be
made acquainted with 100's security in 360's friendship without
knowing the reason of it. To conclude, remember how much the
secret in the matter imports (involves) 386 and take care that no

[1] mpsebswoefmm = Lord Arundell.
[2] The decoded text is on page 138.

new body be acquainted with it till I see what 340 brings 334 in answer to his propositions. I would fain know which I cannot do but by 336 how ready 323 is to break with 299. That is the game that would, as I conceive, most accommodate the interests of both 270 and 297.'

A draft document was produced in December 1669, originally prepared by Clifford—who knew no French—and translated by Sir Richard Bellings. It was full of corrections and marginal notes— the work of several days by Arlington and Clifford, with Bellings acting as secretary. Its demands were extravagant and were no doubt intended to be. A higher price was asked for English friendship than Louis was prepared to pay. The subsequent compromise reflected something nearer reality for both sides.

The busy two years culminated in the visit of Madame, who set sail from Dunkirk on 26 May 1670. She and her retinue of over two hundred and fifty landed at Dover. Charles II was at last united with his dear Minette. It was a joyous occasion, bringing some gaiety into her young life. The marriage with Monsieur had not been happy. When he wasn't being rude to her, he ignored her. Recently pain had racked her for hours at a time. She tired easily.

Her part in the negotiations was all but over. She had been the intermediary between Louis and Charles; she had been allowed to discuss the affair with others; she had smoothed the path of events rather than dictated their course. On 12 June Madame sailed back to France. Before the month was out she had died, probably of acute appendicitis, at Versailles. Like Charles's own wife Catherine she had been a virtuous woman. He lost the companion of his exile[1] and the correspondent of his reign. Thereafter history has no direct access to the record of Charles's innermost thoughts.

THE TREATY OF DOVER

The secret treaty of Dover was signed on 1 June by Arlington, Arundell, Clifford and Bellings for England and Colbert de Croissy for France. Colbert de Croissy took one copy to France, where

---

[1] It had been a brief companionship. When they met again in 1659 he did not recognize her. By 1660 he was away in England. They never met again until 1670.

Louis XIV ratified it in a separate letter. Subsequently both kings exchanged letters of ratification. The other copy found its way to Ugbrooke Park, Chudleigh, the Devon home of the Clifford family where, with much other relevant material, it still is.

As the cornerstone of Charles's foreign policy the treaty deserves close examination.[1] By it, Charles and Louis agreed in the first article upon a union and friendship which was to be inviolable, and 'beyond the capacity of anything in the world to disturb it'.

In the second article, Charles II, 'being convinced of the truth of the Catholic religion', 'resolved to declare it as soon as the welfare of his kingdom will permit'. While doubting that his subjects 'will ever fail in the obedience that all peoples owe to their sovereigns', there is nevertheless an assurance that Louis XIV, as an 'unquestionable proof of the reality of his friendship and to contribute to the success of so glorious a design' of service to the whole Catholic religion, will give Charles II £140,000, half on ratification and half in three months' time. Furthermore, Louis bound himself to provide transport and pay for 6000 troops if Charles needed them 'for the execution of his design'. Fourthly, 'the time of the said declaration of Catholicism' was left entirely to Charles.

The second article of the treaty was the religious one. There are three important points. The declaration of Charles's Catholicism, the offer of aid to its enforcement, and the timing of such a declaration to be in Charles's hands.

It is a fine point, but Charles may just be excused from binding himself to restore the country to Catholicism, as opposed to restoring himself to the Faith. Charles had all through 1669–70 hoped that he might be able to have some control over the time at which war would break out against the Dutch. By declaring his religious conversion first of all, he secured this control. In the event it was a meaningless arrangement, and when they met Madame persuaded him (if he needed much persuasion) that he must delay his declaration.

The third article bound Louis XIV to keep the peace with Spain and not contravene the treaty of Aix-la-Chapelle. In that way Charles could continue to abide by the Triple Alliance. As long as possible

[1] The full text is on page 166.

Charles and Arlington preserved the fiction that the Triple Alliance was secure.

The fourth article committed Charles to helping Louis 'if there should hereafter fall to (him) any new titles and rights to the Spanish monarchy'. In other words, the death of the Spanish Charles II would be the occasion for the English Charles to help Louis. How differently events turned out thirty years later when both Charles's were dead!

The fifth article declared their resolution 'to humble the pride' of the Dutch, a nation which had 'so often rendered itself odious by extreme ingratitude' to those who had helped it into existence. Charles and Louis agreed to make war on the Dutch, forbid trade with them, and annul all treaties with them except for the Triple Alliance.

The sixth and seventh articles contained details concerning the raising and transport of troops to fight the Dutch, and allowed Louis XIV to bear most of the cost, Charles 'only to contribute' six thousand troops. England had the greater responsibility at sea in the forthcoming war. Nevertheless Louis still assumed the major financial responsibility and agreed to pay Charles £210,000 in instalments. The article also specified Charles's gains in the event of victory. Charles was limited to 'the island of Walcheren, Sluys and the island of Cadsand' as his spoils of victory. Thirdly, they sought to do all they could to ensure that William of Orange might 'find his advantage in the continuation and end of the war'.

The details of precedence and responsibility in the naval aspects of the war were worked out with some care. It shows Charles's determination to uphold the prestige of his navy. By contrast, a reference to William of Orange, whose interests were important if the rule of de Witt fell, was vague in the extreme. Louis, who was paying the piper, was also calling the tune.

The eighth article indicated their intention to bring Sweden and Denmark into the war against the Dutch, 'or at least oblige them to remain neutral'. Help was also to be sought from the bishop of Munster, and they would do their utmost to persuade the Austrian and Spanish Habsburgs not to oppose the conquest of the Netherlands. There is a complete contradiction of the intent to preserve the Triple Alliance in the proposal to bring Sweden in against the Dutch.

The ninth article stated that once Charles had made his religious declaration 'which it is hoped will be followed with good success', the moment when war would be declared on the Dutch would be decided by Louis XIV, whereupon Charles 'must make his declaration of war conjointly'.

So it was to be a declaration of religious intent by Charles, followed by a declaration of war by Louis—in that order. In the event the declaration of war came first and the declaration of religious intent not at all. This no doubt had always been Charles's intended strategy. The reverse (war second) was a fiction which deceived Louis, Madame and Clifford all along.

The tenth article nullified any existing treaties 'with any prince or state' inconsistent with this one, and concluded by saying that England and France should make a 'treaty of commerce as soon as possible'.

The treaty of commerce, about which Charles had been so insistent to Madame, was now tucked away in the last article, and never implemented. 'The thing which is nearest the heart of this nation is trade,' Charles had once said. In this respect, Dover—secret or *simulé*—failed him.

Such was the secret treaty of Dover. It was the high-water mark of Charles's personal foreign policy. Its creation had been his major concern during a particularly active period of his public life. Its consequences were both immediate—a Dutch war—and long-term. It might have cost him his throne. It helped to deprive James II of his instead. Controversy has surrounded Charles's motives and challenged his sincerity. It is therefore worthwhile looking briefly at the historiography of the subject. What have some historians thought about the secret treaty?

Lord Macaulay[1] placed first Charles's determination to rid himself of parliament with the aid of the French king. And so he descended 'to the rank of a great vassal', forced to 'make peace and war according to the direction of the government which protected him'. In

[1] *History of England*, 1848 and *Critical Essays*, 1843.

Macaulay's view this did not distress a king 'destitute of all patriotism', who sought the money to gratify his private tastes. 'For these ends, and for these ends alone, he wished to obtain arbitrary power.' It is a damning judgement by the great Victorian Whig historian.

Von Ranke,[1] the German historian who like Macaulay was in the tradition of great narrators of history, saw a lack of logic in the Dover treaty: 'How could a despotic crown join with one established to carry out the system of parliamentary government?' he asked.

Osmond Airy,[2] the first important biographer of Charles II, was bitterly critical of the Dover policy. Writing at the turn of the century, and again in the tradition of Victorian Protestant scholarship, he saw Charles as neutralizing 'the opinion of free and Protestant England' and enlisting French support 'in the interests of despotism and Catholicism'. For Airy 'bloodshed and desolation began at Dover and ended at Utrecht'.

G. M. Trevelyan,[3] Macaulay's great nephew, was equally critical. He continued to offer the view of the Whig critics, which triumphed over any would-be apologists for Charles.

Historians writing in the 1920s and 1930s took varying attitudes. A. S. Turberville[4] believed that Charles secured a valuable ally against the commercial rivalry of the Dutch.

Sir Keith Feiling[5] saw the religious aspects of Dover as subsidiary to the political ones. Charles II, whose abilities Feiling did not doubt, nevertheless 'put England at the mercy of Louis XIV'. The country was committed to war with the Dutch certainly in the French interest, more problematically in the English.

Sir Arthur Bryant[6] was more sympathetic to Charles as a whole. But a significant sentence indicated the stark reality of events for Charles: 'lonely and desperate as was the game Charles had chosen, his every move showed how well fitted he was to play it'. Charles was a man of tolerance, and Bryant found this a factor in the king's favour in the religious aspects of the Dover negotiations.

---

[1] *A History of England, principally in the seventeenth century*, 1875.
[2] *Charles II*, 1901.   [3] *England under the Stuarts*, 1904.
[4] *Commonwealth and Restoration*, 1928.   [5] *British Foreign Policy 1660–72*, 1930.
[6] *Charles II*, 1931.

C. H. Hartmann[1] offered the most favourable view. He recognized that Charles used religion as a means to an end, although conceding the king's undoubted preference for Catholicism. But the end, an alliance with France, with entirely justifiable Anglo-French co-operation, the union of great naval and military powers respectively against the continuing naval and military challenge of Holland, was in England's best interests. Holland was England's natural enemy.

David Ogg,[2] though writing broadly in the older tradition of Caroline critics, saw war against the Dutch as a 'legitimate development in English policy'. If they had been finally defeated, English colonial and commercial expansion could have proceeded unmolested by the United Provinces. In judging Charles II on the intellectual success of his actions rather than on their morality, Ogg (just) came down on Charles's side in the Dover affair.

Sir George Clark[3] commented on the risks that Charles ran if his plans had become known. The king would have met with 'fierce antipathy', which would have divided the realm.

Maurice Ashley,[4] the latest biographer of Charles II, after a gap of forty years, is moderately favourable towards the king's conduct. He dismissed both admiration for Louis XIV and need for his money as reasons for the alliance. Charles, in Ashley's view, believed that it was better to oppose Holland than France for commercial reasons, while ensuring also that the two countries did not themselves come together.

So have historians viewed the controversies of a drama which ended in June 1670. Charles II spent the late summer holidaying at Windsor and at Newmarket. There was Madame's death to get over—'my grief for her is so great that I dare not allow myself to dwell upon it'—and the pleasure of watching Queen Catherine fishing. While he played, others went about his business for him. Buckingham—omitted from the signatories of June and ignorant of the treaty—was in France negotiating a treaty of alliance with Louis. It was an occasion to bring in Charles's other ministers, whose

[1] *Charles II and Madame*, 1934, and *The King, my brother*, 1954.
[2] *England in the reign of Charles II*, 1934.
[3] *The Later Stuarts*, 1934.
[4] *Charles II*, 1971.

initials rather than their solidarity made them the 'Cabal'. Clifford and Arlington were in on the secret; Buckingham was being flattered with the responsibility of negotiating a treaty with Louis— no wonder Molière could write upon the artificiality of men's behaviour in seventeenth-century France; Ashley and Lauderdale, two stout Protestants, would also sign the new document, which was drawn up on 21 December 1670 and became known to history as the treaty *simulé*. It omitted the second article of the secret treaty. The cash payment mentioned in article two now appeared in the text of the original article seven—as an additional war-payment. The declaration of war indicated in the original article nine was fixed for the spring of 1672, with the religious clauses deleted. Charles and the Cabal were ready to go to war with the Dutch: 'our business is to break with them and yet to lay the breach at their door', said Arlington. Not for the first time in the seventeenth century, England was to be the undoubted aggressor.

PARLIAMENT AND WAR

Parliament had played little part in events since the fall of Clarendon. To some extent Charles had yielded to its cry for his impeachment, though he was glad the old man escaped. Clarendon's exile however did nothing to improve Charles's relations with the Commons, and only one of the men with whom he dealt in the committee for foreign affairs was in the Lower House. Certainly, as we have seen, the desire to end his financial subservience to parliament was a factor in Charles's 'Dover' policy, and we may briefly notice his relations with that body between 1667 and the outbreak of war.

After a long recess (May 1668–October 1669) he found the Commons as interested in their privileges as their ancestors had been. The privilege case of Skinner *v*. The East India Company was more important to them than the financial obligations Charles had incurred by entering the Triple Alliance and strengthening the navy. Charles prorogued parliament from December 1669 till February 1670. When next it met, in the short session of February–April 1670, relations were better. The Commons were far from unmanageable, and the influence of the Court was still strong. Charles was able to assure them that the money previously voted for the second Anglo-Dutch war had not 'been diverted to other purposes'. They parted on 11 April 1670 'well satisfied with their meeting'. Nevertheless Charles, as ever, remained short of money.

When the Commons assembled again in October 1670—while Buckingham was negotiating the treaty *simulé*—they voted Charles money for the upkeep of the navy. The bargain he struck with them was a callous one—the eviction of Jesuits and Roman priests from England. His known leniency to Catholics had encouraged their activities, and rumours that something sinister had happened at Dover were beginning to circulate.

Such a decision made Charles realize he would be in a better position to carry out the implications of his post-Dover policy without parliament. The parliament that stood prorogued in April 1671 had shown sufficient hostility to Charles's incipient Catholicism for him to dispense with its services for, as it turned out, twenty-two months. Charles, acting with that prerogative authority which the Stuart kings exercised in the conduct of foreign policy, committed England to war against the Dutch on 28 March 1672. No declaration in favour of Catholicism preceded the declaration of war. An excuse for war had readily been found, by claiming insult to the flag when Sir William Temple's wife, Dorothy Osborne, was returning home, and a Dutch merchant fleet and its escort was deliberately provoked in the English Channel. It was a lame if adequate excuse.

On the eve of war Charles II seemed to have every prospect of victory. Clifford had devised a way to give him more money, by suggesting that the crown withhold the repaying of capital and interest on sums borrowed from the goldsmiths—the scheme was known as the Stop of the Exchequer. The Dutch were unprepared for war. They lacked troops in readiness, since the burgher-regents feared the idea of a standing army. John de Witt and the States-General ignored repeated reports of French military movements. Only their navy was in any sort of condition for war. Economically the rout of the Dutch would be a major stimulus to English trade, while politically Charles could place his nephew William on such Dutch territory as he and Louis chose to leave independent. In this euphoria he elevated the men who had helped him—a dukedom in the Scottish peerage for Lauderdale, earldoms for Arlington and Ashley, and a barony for Clifford, who thus left the Commons. Charles was—though he did not realize it—bringing about the end of the Cabal. When Ashley became the Earl of Shaftesbury the word 'Cabal' could no longer be formed. More significantly the king issued a Declaration of Indulgence suspending penal laws against dissenters and Roman Catholics. It was a measure of self-confidence; it would please Louis XIV; it reflected his own inclinations; it would 'keep all quiet at home whilst we are busiest abroad', as Arlington wrongly surmised.

England's entry into the third Anglo-Dutch war is not an event in which to take pride. The Commons had not in 1671 intended that public money be used against the Dutch; the Triple Alliance was being violated; the ruthless ambitions—economic and political—of Colbert and Louis XIV were being bolstered. Yet the country itself was ambivalent: to fight the Dutch had become traditional to Englishmen of all ages. In 1672 you had to be aged eighty-two to remember Anglo-Dutch co-operation against the Spaniard.

Furthermore, the Dutch were dealing economic blows in English coastal waters—attacking fishing vessels off the East Anglian coast and intercepting colliers sailing down the North Sea to London. These had their effect on domestic prices. On the other hand, French armies were afoot and 'all Protestant hearts trembled', while Colbert's fiscal policies in France were also affecting the English economy. Who was the real enemy?

The war was fought by land and sea. As the treaty of Dover had envisaged, France bore the brunt of the military attack on the Dutch, while England's navy led the campaign by sea. Condé and Turenne swept through the Netherlands with 120,000 men, approaching Amsterdam, while hastily-mustered Dutchmen fell back before them. The Dutch command had been given, by popular acclaim, to Prince William of Orange, and his decisive order to cut the dykes created a vast morass of water which stayed the French advance and devastated Dutch homesteads.

At sea the Dutch task was a defensive one. De Ruyter had to prevent an Anglo-French fleet landing forces. Turning defence into attack, de Ruyter attacked his enemy in Southwold Bay off the

Suffolk coast in June 1672, burning the English flagship, the *Royal James*, and preventing the success of a naval expeditionary force. Southwold Bay was a disaster of some magnitude. The English admiral, Lord Sandwich, was drowned in the explosion of the *Royal James*. The Duke of York lost two hundred men in the *Prince*, but himself survived by transferring to another vessel. Charles II made the funeral of Sandwich a great occasion at Westminster Abbey. De Ruyter had done his part effectively, but French troops ruthlessly advanced. Louis and Charles sent Dutch embassies for peace away empty-handed.

In the flurry of defeat Dutchmen turned on Dutchmen. The de Witt brothers narrowly escaped assassination in June, only to be brutally murdered in August. Even while John de Witt was defending himself against accusations trumped up by a desperate Estates-General, fresh negotiations had been entered into with Louis XIV. The terms he offered smacked of Adolf Hitler's policies in the 1930s. If accepted, there would have been no sovereign Dutch nation. Charles II's reply was equally ruthless, and his nephew William cried: 'Let us be hacked in pieces, than accept such conditions.'

Here was the new leader—stadtholder, captain and admiral-general. He had taken a line his uncle had not expected. He was a hero in all respects save one: the men who murdered the de Witts were unpunished and even rewarded. Another Orange ruler, Maurice, had served the memory of Oldenbarneveldt equally harshly. But the man had arrived who was ultimately to end the Stuart dynasty.

In 1673 the war swung the other way. William, fighting all through the preceding winter, kept the French at bay with his defensive water-line. Spanish and Austrian troops joined him in defeating a French army at Bonn in November 1673. By Christmas the enemy had been driven out of the United Provinces. De Ruyter had done his share at sea. The English had been held back at the mouth of the Scheldt in June—a year to the day after Southwold Bay—and a victory off Texel in August finally ended any prospect of a naval invasion.

Louis XIV was not so easily repulsed, but the new Dutch stadtholder sought to end the war with England, and concluded in February

1674 the peace of Westminster. The Dutch at last agreed to strike their flags to English vessels between Finisterre and Norway, and paid a war indemnity. New York, captured in the war, was returned to England. The terms of the treaty mattered less than the sequel. Parliamentary reaction to the war had its repercussions on Charles and his ministers.

During the first year of the war parliament had not met. As we saw, it had stood prorogued since April 1671. When it met again in February 1673, its first action was to challenge Shaftesbury's right, as lord chancellor, to issue writs for by-elections to fill vacant seats. This was a Commons' privilege, and some new members had to leave the chamber. Shaftesbury's intentions had been to provide crown supporters. Charles defended 'a necessary and expensive war' to an unimpressed parliament, who faced two unpleasant facts: a war at sea in which the English had fared badly; and the suspension of all penal laws against 'whatsoever sort of nonconformists or recusants'. Only so far had Charles II been prepared to go in meeting the secret and public terms of his treaties with Louis.

The Commons' reaction was to vote a reluctant £1,260,000 (over three years) to aid a war of whose objectives they were thoroughly suspicious. There was 'something to hide', as even such a good royalist as Sir Giles Strangeways observed. As for the Declaration of Indulgence, Charles was told he had made a 'mistake' —more charitable criticism than his father received. The Declaration was withdrawn by the king and countered by the Test Act, which firmly wedded Anglicanism to the State and statutorily banned from public office those who refused the sacraments of the Church of England. Mercifully for the good name of Anglicanism and for the cause of religion as a whole, it was less rigidly enforced by later generations. Nevertheless it remained the law of the land until the nineteenth century, and its implications survive into our own times.[1]

The Test Act caused the resignations of the Duke of York and Lord Clifford, from the admiralty and treasury respectively. York's office was put into commission and one of its incidental consequences was to bring Samuel Pepys to the office of secretary to the admiralty

---

[1] The selection committee who interviewed Duff Cooper in 1924 for a parliamentary constituency wished to be assured he was not a Roman Catholic.

board. Charles II had appointed a man as devoted to the navy as he was himself.

Parliament was by now thoroughly convinced that the French alliance should be equated with popery, and viewed with no enthusiasm the Duke of York's marriage to a young Italian princess, Mary of Modena. James and Mary might well become the parents of a future Catholic king.

Almost in the fashion of the first half of the century the Commons debated their grievances: money for Charles was money for more war; there was a danger of a standing army; the king was beset by evil counsellors; popery was rife. The time had come to curb Charles's policies and bring down the Cabal. Clifford had already gone, and died at his Dartmoor home before the year was out. Shaftesbury was dismissed from the lord chancellorship in November 1673, and was already planning to play a new part in public life in opposition. Charles had made his peace with the Dutch by February 1674 and needed his parliament no more. He prorogued it that same month. But he was not without caution. Buckingham was dismissed from his service, Arlington given a dignified but lesser portfolio as lord chamberlain, and Lauderdale allowed to remain master in Scotland. But Sir Charles Wheeler had the last word as he muttered in the Commons 'Why shall not this parliament be a precedent to future parliaments, as well as former parliaments to this?' For us, it poses the question of how near had England come to another civil conflict in 1674?

City men accused Charles of laziness, of avoiding that 'impertinent thing called business'. Politicians had taken up the cudgels of an earlier generation. But the cudgels were verbal ones: no man was ready to fight the king. Charles had given way with a reasonable grace, while one of his Cabal was emerging as a leader of an opposition acquiring the respectabillity of a 'party'. Shaftesbury was creating Whiggism. In the end Whig doctrine acclaimed the political and constitutional circumstances that deprived Charles's brother of this throne. But in 1674 Charles had nothing to fear. His executive of the past seven years was gone, and in a way he was not sorry to see it go. Its solidarity had always resided in the fiction rather than the fact of a Cabal. This was a weakness which

K

made it easier for the Commons to destroy it. By then Charles's new minister was already treasurer of the navy. Sir Thomas Osborne, Earl of Danby, had come to power. If he had a lineal ancestor in the Cabal, it was Buckingham.

★   ★   ★

Letter written by Charles II to Madame, 7 June 1669:[1]

'Upon the whole matter I see no kind of necessity of telling Colbert de Croissy of the secret now, nor indeed till England is in a better readiness to make use of France towards the great business. It will be enough that Colbert de Croissy be acquainted with Louis XIV's security in Charles II's friendship without knowing the reason of it. To conclude, remember how much the secret in the matter imports (involves) Charles II and take care that no new body be acquainted with it till I see what Arundell brings Charles II in answer to his propositions. I would fain know which I cannot do but by Arundell how ready France is to break with Holland. That is the game that would, as I conceive, most accommodate the interests both of England and France.'

[1] See page 125.

10 A kingdom in disarray, 1674–88

'French and papists, two terms of art in every malicious mouth, completing revenge on whomsoever either can be pinned, and considering the very credulity of this uncharitable age, it seldom fails to stick'

Colonel Edward Cooke

DANBY: PARLIAMENT AND POLICIES

The man who succeeded Clifford as lord treasurer in June 1673 was too young to have served in the Civil War, and too obscure to have been rewarded with office at the Restoration. His chance of promotion in public life came with the fall of Clarendon and the opportunity then given for new men to rise to power. He served a valuable apprenticeship as treasurer of the navy, made friends with City business men, disliked what he heard about the 'Dover' policies, and became a privy councillor in the general distribution of favours in 1672.

Osborne's efficiency made him enemies in an age when public men disliked the scrutiny of officialdom. He was a friend and colleague of Pepys and had some of the inquisitiveness of the diarist. His appointment to the lord treasurership was not popular. He had, Charles told him, two friends, the king and his own talents. If his brief was to balance the books in favour of Charles, few envied him or expected him to last. As events turned out, Thomas Osborne served Charles until 1679, and subsequently was in and out of public life right up to his death just before the arrival of the first Hanoverian, with whom he was in correspondence about the succession as late as 1710. He was steadily advanced in the English peerage, being created in turn Baron Osborne, Viscount Latimer, Earl of Danby, Marquis of Carmarthen and Duke of Leeds. Posterity knows him but as Danby.

In domestic politics Danby's rôle was clear: to grapple with crown finances and to secure a majority for the court party in the House of Commons. It was the stringency of his economies and the efficiency of his accounting which put Charles's affairs in some semblance of order. His skill in organization was shown in the way he built up a coherent and well-disciplined court party. His immediate part in foreign policies was less evident. His sympathies were not with the crown's French policy—and Charles knew this. Yet as the king's minister he was forced into a certain identification with what Charles did. In the end this proved his undoing, at the hands of parliament. Fundamentally Danby held the view that a good relationship between king and parliament depended upon a pro-Dutch foreign policy. He believed that such a relationship might emerge if he could assure Charles of reasonable financial security and woo him from his French sympathies. Only by supporting the cause of the Dutch against the French aggression might Charles hope to 'fall into the humours of his people'.

It was to be Danby's tragedy that men forgot his efforts for Anglo-Dutch relations—such as bringing about the marriage of William and Mary in 1677—and remembered his association with Charles's French intrigues, in particular his connivance at the secret treaty made between the two kings in 1676.

To the question of why did Charles employ Danby as his principal minister in these years, one may make four answers: he was a hard worker; he was business-like with money; he could manage the House of Commons; and his king was astute enough to realize the public value of a minister in sympathy with more popular alternative foreign policies. Danby saved Charles from the worst excesses in his pro-French policy, and in doing so helped to keep the king on his throne.

The interaction between parliamentary attitudes and the crown's foreign policy, of which Danby was so aware, emerges in a brief examination of parliamentary affairs and French reaction between 1675 and 1679.

Parliament in these four years met in fits and starts, and it was prorogued by Charles when concessions were insufficient or hostility rampant. Thus the sessions of April to June and October to

November of 1675 ended because Charles was asked to withdraw English troops from French service and because he only received about two-thirds of what he sought for shipbuilding. Two further factors were the privilege case, between Lords and Commons, of Shirley *v.* Fagg (1675) and the attempts of some members to bring down both Danby and Lauderdale. But the main importance of these months was the increasing polarization of 'court' and 'country' factions. Danby, by the use of bribery and influence, had won a measure of support for Charles. Shaftesbury, using cheaper methods (in both senses), was creating an opposition which was encouraged to fear popery and force a general election that would return an anti-French House of Commons.

A gap of fifteen months after November 1675 was followed by a series of sessions between February 1677 and January 1679 which brought to an end Charles's 'Cavalier' Parliament. The financial policy of these two years is a reflection on parliamentary policy towards Charles as a whole. There were three major monetary grants: the first a generous one of £600,000 for the navy, the second so tightly appropriated that it was of little direct use to Charles, and the third primarily directed towards paying off the army. A parliament summoned in 1661 as the bulwark of a restored monarchy now found itself dissolved after eighteen years. At its dissolution it was a prey to suspicions, bribes, and a wholesome fear of an army in the king's hands.

Louis XIV's reaction to parliamentary activity in the years 1675 to 1679 was to offer Charles the promise—if not always the substance—of French money. After the session of 1675 for example Charles received a grudging payment of £100,000, which was given unenthusiastically in instalments because he had not met Louis's wishes and because Louis had already spent £100,000 trying to bribe support and so spread confusion in the Commons. With Danby's generosity thrown in—and Dutch offerings for good measure—the members could be forgiven for wondering on whom to confer their favours. Assuredly they did not confer them on Charles—nor indeed on Louis, who wanted English aid at best, and English neutrality at worst. He had lost Marshal Turenne in battle, while his Swedish allies had been defeated at Fehrbellin.

As the Spanish had found in the 1570s the Dutch were not 'men of butter' to be beaten at will. Louis really wanted Charles to dissolve parliament rather than prorogue it, but Charles was not yet prepared to become so totally dependent upon Danby's efficiency and Louis's generosity, added to which there was the prospect of a general election returning a less sympathetic parliament dominated by Shaftesbury.

In the period 1677–9 French money found its way into Charles's hands as further rewards for not breaking with France at parliament's request, while a sum of £500,000—scarcely earned—came for negotiating the Nymegen peace settlement. While Charles well and truly milched his French cousin, and since French money was also passing into the hands of the Commons, one may ask if Louis XIV got value for money by his distribution of largesse. By bribing Charles he ensured parliamentary adjournments—but not a dissolution till 1679. By bribing members of parliament he frustrated the prospects of an English entry into the war—only a serious possibility after the treaty Danby negotiated with the Dutch following the marriage of William and Mary in 1677. By bribing both sides he made his contribution to the breakdown of all trust in public men and public positions that characterizes the last years of the king's reign. If Louis sought to lower the credibility of English government, he spent his money well. If he sought to win an ally, it was money down the drain. But let him have the last word—he could afford it!

Charles had attempted mediation between French and Dutch within weeks of his withdrawal from the war in February 1674. He employed Temple somewhat fruitlessly in the summer and Arlington in the winter. Nothing emerged except the first suggestions of a marriage between William of Orange and Mary. In 1675 Temple was again in the Netherlands, where Charles had sent him to Nymegen to set up peace negotiations. Temple surveyed the geography of the war, and produced lists of places which should be retained or conceded by France in order that a Flanders frontier might be established. Both French and Dutch rejected them; Charles's overtures had failed.

What were the king's motives? Mediation was a public gesture which his critics could note with approval. Its success might make him the honest broker in resolving Franco-Dutch rivalries. More realistically, as Charles confessed to Temple, parliament would never leave him alone 'while the war lasted abroad'. But Charles had little claim on the protagonists, and their eventual settlement, in the peace of Nymegen, owed little to him, despite the ever-present Temple, whose contribution in 1678 was to stop undue French territorial greed in the interests of her ally Sweden. Nations which opt out of a continuing war have no rôle when victors and vanquished assemble. Charles II in 1678 was of far less importance than Louis XIV or William of Orange. For the rest of his reign, it may be agreed, his foreign policy neither damaged nor enhanced English interests. The treaty of Nymegen in July 1678 ended six years of war between France and Holland. The French gained Franche-Comté and ate into Spanish Flanders. Louis XIV's graph of military triumphs was to continue climbing until 1697.

There would be two more parliaments in Charles's reign, between 1679 and 1681, and then Charles bade farewell to parliament men for ever: 'I will not yield, nor will I be bullied. Men usually become more timid as they become older; it is the opposite with me.' There was bitterness in those two years, but the real seeds of mistrust had been sown between 1675 and 1679.

Why did king mistrust parliament, and parliament mistrust king? The basis of their division was foreign policy. The Commons, which had forced the end of the third Anglo-Dutch war, more and more looked towards the Dutch as allies, on both political and commercial grounds. Politically the Dutch made an appeal to Englishmen, thanks to the propaganda used by William of Orange, in particular the pamphlet *England's Appeal from the Private Cabal to the Great Council of the Nation* (1673). There were already those who saw him as the possible Protestant successor to the throne, especially after his marriage in 1677 to Mary, James's elder—and Protestant—daughter. Others, looking for a domestic and legitimate solution, wanted Charles to divorce Catherine, marry again and beget a Protestant heir. Charles, it is true, had acquiesced in the Dutch marriage, but his policy in this instance was a departure from his overall identification with France.

Commercially, rivalry with the Dutch was now of less account compared with the economic challenge of Colbert's policies in France. French mercantilist pursuits were damaging English fiscal, trading and shipping interests, although the historian must proceed with caution in establishing a connection between the commercial decline of the Dutch and the expansion of English trade after the 1670s. It was not so much that contemporary Englishmen saw a Dutch decline, but that they became aware of French economic growth. This lay behind the determination of many of them to accept the Dutch as partners in world trade and to encourage Dutch investment in England.

These were positive reasons for tacking towards the Dutch. There were equally convincing political and commercial ones for veering away from the French, whose successes in 1677 for example threatened to put Spanish Flanders under French domination. Danby realized this, and commented that 'men's fears are grown both so general and so great' that the king could no longer allow himself to be seen as so markedly pro-French.

To be pro-French and to be pro-Catholic: these were further causes of parliamentary mistrust, which Charles could only allay by positive commitments to war with France and support for Anglicanism. Danby realized the need for an entrenched Anglican position (as he showed in encouraging an Order in Council against Catholics in 1675). This was as important as a foreign policy in sympathy with the Dutch. It is a curiosity of the king's government in these years that it seemed to be pursuing rival courses with mutual consent. Both king and Danby knew what the other was about.

Englishmen in the 1670s were made aware of the French threat to English commerce. Colbert was demonstrating mercantilist policies at their most aggressive. Tariff duties penalized English ships in French ports; government-subsidized textile industries in France hit the textile industry in England, causing depression at several social levels and in various geographical areas; colonial incursions in the West Indies and India damaged well-established English interests. All this was a matter of concern to the House of Commons, especially after 1674 when economic retaliation against the French was discussed. By 1678 parliament had forbidden the importation of a large range of French luxury goods, including silks and wines. There was an acute awareness of being at an economic disadvantage compared with France, at a time when Charles II was known to be in constant secret dialogue with Barillon, the French ambassador. It was a major factor in parliamentary mistrust of the king.

Although the furtiveness of Charles's activities contributed towards distrust, he had no option. If the full extent of his dealings with Louis had been known, his monarchy might not have survived. Temple warned him of the dangers as early as 1674. Charles placated Temple—'I will be the man of my people'—but he also placated the French ambassador in the same month.

What of Charles's mistrust of parliament? This suggests another aspect to their relationship. Charles was convinced that parliament was trying to force him to embark upon a war against France which he did not want and which the Commons would not pay for. He recognized that it was only the view of a part of the Commons. In May 1677 for instance 182 members out of 324 present asked the king 'to enter into a league, offensive and defensive, with the United Provinces'. But whether part of the Commons, or all of it—and Danby's bribes reduced the opposition—it was none of their business to challenge the prerogative in matters of war and peace. Charles spoke firmly to the House on that occasion, but softened his criticism eight months later, in January 1678, when he told them he was concerned for the safety of Flanders and was trying to secure an honourable peace. But Charles the mediator was insufficiently credit-worthy for the Commons. Whatever might have been his earlier failings—he had got himself embroiled in the mesh of French ambitions in the 1660s—he was now in 1678 making an attempt to contribute to the peace of Europe. But when the treaty of Nymegen was signed, it owed little, as we have seen, to Charles's or Temple's contribution.

EXCLUSION AND APPEASEMENT

Three weeks after the ratification of the treaty of Nymegen, the first whispers reached Charles of a scare that was shortly to engulf the nation: The Popish plot. Briefly, Titus Oates and Israel

Tonge swore before a magistrate, Sir Edmund Berry Godfrey, that there was a Jesuit plot to assassinate Charles II, murder Protestants and put James on the throne. Subsequently the body of Godfrey was found pierced by a sword. No convincing explanation emerged of this tragedy, but it led to mass hysteria. Protestants such as Godfrey were to be murdered as they went their way. Oates, already a known perjurer, had gained fame—if that was what he sought. For nearly three years the political implications of the plot brought terror to Catholics, of whom some thirty-five were executed, including one peer and the archbishop of Armagh, Oliver Plunket, and it created an undoubted threat to James's chances of succeeding to the throne. His possible exclusion dominated domestic politics for the remainder of the reign, while the wider issue of succession remained open until 1714. One immediate consequence was the fall of Danby. Any connection between the Popish plot and the king's minister was thin in the extreme, but parliamentary opposition forces had made the most of the plot to try to rid themselves of James, Duke of York. Danby stood by the duke and succeeded in exempting him from the act of 1678 to exclude all Roman Catholics from parliament. But the effective attack against the king's minister came from another quarter. Ralph Montague, who had served as an ambassador in Paris, disclosed two letters from Danby to him asking for a subsidy to be obtained from Louis XIV to keep England out of the war. Montagu had various grudges against Danby—including a refusal to allow him to buy office, as secretary of state—and sought an opportunity to settle old scores. On 20 December 1678, Montague—protected from arrest by securing membership of the Commons—asked leave of the Speaker to perform 'a painful duty'. The House was full of men ready to condemn Danby for high treason, but there were others who defended him. Sir Thomas Higgons argued that kings might ask one another for money as a condition of remaining neutral—Henry VII had done it. Sir John Birkenhead chided Montagu with misprision of treason for holding on to the evidence for so long. Sir John Ernle asked Montague how he had replied to the letters. It was enough to procure Danby's eventual fall, but it also toppled the 'Cavalier' parliament.

The king was determined to save his minister from the fate Strafford had met. A new parliament was elected hostile to the court. Shaftesbury himself reckoned the 'opposition' numbered over 300, as against 150 or so who supported the 'court'. Its business with Danby was soon settled. The Commons brought in a bill of attainder and invalidated Charles's pardon—given by the king because the disgraced minister had been acting in Charles's interests and against his own inclinations. It was to Charles's credit that he defended Danby; to his discredit that he let him be committeed to the Tower of London. There Danby lingered, without trial or bail, until 1684. Montagu thought it prudent to keep out of Charles's way and departed for the continent until the king's death.

The exclusion crisis made Charles II largely a spectator in foreign affairs between 1679 and 1684, while Louis XIV pursued a policy of aggression. Louis's lawyers, through the Chambres de Réunion, dug out medieval claims to various fiefdoms which they said should have been in French hands. His soldiers moved in to settle the argument. What law could not establish nor force secure, money might buy. In these ways the eastern frontiers of France were strengthened through penetration into Alsace, Luxemburg, Strasburg and northern Italy. Meanwhile, his ambassador at The Hague, Count D'Avaux, encouraged William of Orange's internal opponents, and this weakened Dutch resistance to Louis.

The climax of these particular years was the Diet of Ratisbon (1684), when Louis XIV paused for breath. The major powers and he made a twenty-year truce which confirmed Louis's ill-gotten gains so far. No one believed it would last, least of all Louis. By 1704—its date of expiry—the War of the League of Augsburg was past history, and that of the Spanish Succession current affairs. Louis's successes had been assisted by the attacks the Turks made upon Vienna. The emperor, busy in defending the empire against the infidel, might have hoped for help from Louis XIV. Instead the French king made capital out of these Turkish threats to Christendom. Those who acquiesced in Ratisbon did so in fear and despair. Since Louis XIV's foreign policy was matched in aggression by his domestic one, of persecuting the protestant Huguenots within his own nation, he bid fair to be the dictator of his generation.

And not only Protestants suffered. Protestant and Catholic alike toiled to make possible the ambitions of the king. 'It would be easy to find tyrants more odious than Louis XIV; but there was not one who ever used his power to inflict greater suffering or wrong.' Such was the harsh judgement of the nineteenth-century Catholic historian Lord Acton.[1]

This was the king who was to dominate Europe for a further thirty years after Charles II's death. This was the king to whom Charles II was linked by treaty, financial need, a hint of blackmail and a common acceptance of absolutism in princes. How did England's king react to French policies in the last few years of his life?

Broadly, Charles II took no active part. The retiring French minister, Armand de Pomponne, noted this and delighted in it: a 'perpetually agitated England' suited France best and prevented England from 'making herself considerable abroad'. Charles was a non-participant in events for several reasons. The navy was weak, thanks to the loss of the services of both his brother and Samuel Pepys—in different ways victims of the Popish scare. Naval money was misspent, and the building and maintenance of ships neglected. Foreign policy was regarded as a diversion raised by the king to distract attention from the crisis in domestic policies. He was in no position to finance or prosecute a war against France, especially since he needed Louis; in these final years the French king was of more use to Charles as an insurer than a banker. The money Louis paid was relatively modest and was certainly not sufficient to make Charles credit-worthy. But the French king's support was there—or so Charles believed—if the English throne were to be seriously threatened. This was the basis of Charles's relationship with Louis, and was endorsed in a secret agreement in March 1681.

These were reasons for Charles's non-involvement in Europe. Were they justified? Charles could argue that the course of European events was irrelevant to English interests; that Louis's German policy did not affect England; that Louis would go his own way irrespective of the king of England.

---

[1] In 1972 J. R. Jones wrote: 'French arrogance, the crude bullying and threatening language commonly employed in dealing with minor and virtually defenceless states, was consistent with the general aims of French policy.'

On the other hand by opting out of Europe's affairs Charles posed short and long term difficulties for his country. He had allowed France to threaten both Flanders and the English economy; this was immediately evident. The danger France presented to the balance of power in Europe was also clear within his own lifetime to those—the Empire, Spain, Holland and Sweden—who formed the defensive Quadruple Alliance in 1682.

Yet Charles did not entirely detach himself from European affairs. In 1680 his new minister, Sunderland, explored the possibility of setting up alliances against France. It was a show of strength which deceived no one, and was merely a gesture designed to placate public opinion at home. 'I must pacify the English,' Charles told the French ambassador, Barillon. All that came out of it was a mutual guarantee treaty with Spain. In the following year Charles returned to the rôle of mediator which he had played before Nymegen. Again there were idle threats that he might help the Dutch if French aggression did not cease. Again he gave the game way to Barillon. It was fear of parliament—'they are devils'—which led him to try to restrain Louis's Luxemburg blockade. This was scarcely mediation, though no doubt intended as such. Charles's final effort came in the spring of 1684. He declined to help either the Dutch or the Spanish as an intermediary with Louis, but urged them to make their peace independently with him. It was on a note of appeasement that he concluded the foreign policy of the reign. He welcomed the truce which these nations—and the Empire—reluctantly made at Ratisbon in April 1684. Europe—save for events on the Turkish borders—was at peace. Charles in the final months of his life enjoyed the false idyll of peace abroad and at home. He had stilled his enemies. Shaftesbury had fled to exile and death. The navy was in business again; James[1] and Pepys were once more holding office. He had secured the succession for his brother James, yet had made his peace with his natural son Monmouth. He died in February 1685.

The essence of his foreign policy had been to identify himself with the cause of absolutism in princes: for this reason he had

---

[1] Despite the Test Act.

gravitated towards France. This must be the political theorist's explanation of an attitude which so upset his parliament. That policy was related to the pursuit of Catholic interests. There was an identity between Catholicism and absolutism which all princes in the seventeenth century recognized. But there was a second aspect to Charles's Catholic leanings—an instinct of generosity which made him dislike intolerance, whether to dissenters,[1] regicides or papists. And was there not a third one? Charles on his deathbed chose the sacraments of Rome rather than Canterbury. It was the final moment of sincerity in a man whose virtues and vices alike had led into insincerities.

JAMES II

James II allowed himself no time to formulate a foreign policy. In a reign of just under four years his energies were concentrated on releasing Catholics from the legal restrictions imposed on them. From a political and intellectual angle, James believed the country was being denied, by the Test Act, the use of Catholic talent in such institutions as the services, the universities and the House of Commons. From a religious angle, James saw—far more clearly than most contemporaries wanted to see—an identity between Romanism and Anglicanism. Both might serve the monarchy; only dissenters lent towards republicanism. The monarchy was indeed secure at the death of his brother. Events such as the Rye House plot had brought a reaction in its favour and put Protestant nonconformity into disrepute.

Yet even nonconformists were not beyond redemption. There is considerable evidence to support the view that James was a man of toleration. Gilbert Burnet, indisputably a hostile witness,[2] found him in 1683 'positive in his opinion against all persecution for conscience' sake'. Nor is it surprising to find the king saying in 1687 that 'conscience ought not to be constrained nor people forced in matters of mere religion'. James himself had known political persecution and loss of office in 1673.

These were the premises that led James into pursuing a domestic

[1] The retribution exacted for the Popish Plot must be an exception to this.
[2] See below page 154.

policy on behalf of Catholics from the start of the reign. In the summer of 1685 the ill-fated and pathetic rebellion of his nephew Monmouth ended in the duke's own execution and the ruthless severity of Judge Jeffreys. Monmouth had raised support in the west country, partly from the ranks of Protestant nonconformity and partly from economically depressed employees in the Somerset clothing and mining industries. The rebellion did not represent an attack on the Catholicism of James. But it gave the king some justification for increasing his standing army on Hounslow Heath—and putting in practice his belief that Catholics should be employed in the services. Both factors—the standing army and the employment of Catholics—upset a parliament which he had summoned at the outset of the reign, which he prorogued in November 1685, and which never met again. Meanwhile in August of that same year James had taken one of his few decisions in foreign affairs by renewing existing alliances with the Dutch. It was a gesture of independence flaunted before Louis rather than a positive association with his son-in-law William.

By 1686 the course of James's policy was clear. Catholic talent was not only being used—it was usurping Protestants. At the centre of government were men like Arundell—a signatory of the 'secret' treaty of Dover—and Robert Spencer, Earl of Sunderland, later a temporary convert to Catholicism, but no real friend to James. 'Sunderland', wrote a contemporary, 'had nothing in view but the king's ruin, and the thing showed itself manifestly after.'

More unusually, there was Father Edward Petre. Petre was a baronet and a Jesuit whom James had released from prison and made a privy councillor. Petre, despite the bitter attacks on his name and reputation which followed the departure of James, was a man who counselled caution—advising James, for example, not to have the seven bishops prosecuted in 1688. He got a bad press simply because he was a Jesuit, and the wisdom of James in bringing close to the centre of power a member of an order so hated by English Protestantism may indeed be questioned. More conventional Catholic appointments, as commander of the fleet and lord-lieutenant of Ireland respectively, were Sir Robert Strickland and the Earl of Tyrconnel. Two judicial matters had endorsed this policy of James's: the Godden *v.* Hales (1686) decision in favour of a Catholic officer, and the setting up of a commission for ecclesiastical causes.

It was a policy extended in 1687, when the First Declaration of Indulgence extended the sovereign's prerogative of dispensation of the law into one of suspension. By then James's Catholic policy had penetrated the universities of Oxford and Cambridge and municipal government, while the papal nuncio was received at Windsor.

Europe was at peace and James could safely concentrate on domestic affairs. The formation of the League of Augsburg in 1686 had, he thought, no significance for England. The League, which consisted of the Emperor, Spain, the United Provinces, Sweden and Saxony—joined in 1687 by Bavaria and Savoy—was in fact William of Orange's reply to the threat of French domination of Europe. It was at first defensive only; for it to be aggressive and to tip the balance against Louis, England would have to adhere to it. Though the Pope gave the League secret support, James believed that England's interests would best be served by neutrality in the event of a European war. He never appreciated that English neutrality was useless to William of Orange.

Only in 1688 did James come to realize the potential danger which his son-in-law and daughter presented. In January of that year he tried to recall six English regiments from the Netherlands, but William would only allow officers to go—and they were often Catholics. The Protestant soldiery were kept. By the mid-summer of 1688 James's policy suggested that his throne was in jeopardy and that foreign nations were watching developments in England. Two domestic events in June 1688—one very domestic—had foreign repercussions. The first was the acquittal of the seven bishops, who had been arrested on a technicality for seditious libel. Their 'political' offence had been to reject the Second Declaration of Indulgence by refusing to have it read in their dioceses. The second was the birth of a male heir to James. Mary of Modena was only twenty-nine, but she had had two miscarriages and lost four children in infancy. None had been born for six years. Protestants were confident that the Catholic monarchy would end with James's

death sometime before the end of the seventeenth century.[1] Now
they realized a Catholic monarchy had come to stay unless James
could be overthrown. For that foreign intervention would be
necessary.

Thus the birth of James Stuart—ill-starred infant destined to play
the title rôle in two rebellions against the Hanoverian monarchy,
when he was aged twenty-seven and fifty-seven respectively—
gave immediate impetus to events in England and abroad. Indeed,
within six months the child had begun his life-long exile.

Outside England there were two interested parties: Louis XIV
and William of Orange. The relationship between England and the
countries from which those rulers sprang has dominated a large
part of this book. They provided a seemingly eternal triangle
of differing political alignments. Both rulers had watched events
in England between 1685 and 1688 with some circumspection.
Neither wanted to be closely involved. Louis had got tired of
financing the English monarchy, especially as James in 1685 had
taken some back-pay due to Charles, and—like Oliver Twist—
asked for more. None came after November 1685. During 1686
and 1687 Louis was more concerned with his fortunes in Europe,
using the Ratisbon truce to build vital forts on his eastern frontiers,
intimidate minor German princes, make an alliance with Cologne,
and consider the impact of the League of Augsburg formed by his
rivals in 1686. Not until the summer of 1688 did he make direct
approaches to James through his ambassador, Barillon. Up to
£50,000 was offered for the navy, together with the services of
French shipping. To his credit James received these offers coolly.
If his throne were in danger, he would secure it by concessions to
English Protestant interests rather than by foreign aid. By the
autumn Louis had switched his military interests to central Europe
and sent troops into Germany. In the closing events of James's
reign Louis's rôle in English affairs was confined to offering a home
at St. Germains for the king and his family.

William of Orange had at the outset established good relations
with his father-in-law James. He sent Monmouth away from The

---

[1] James died in 1701 aged sixty-eight.

Hague and gave him no encouragement, telling him to fight the Turks if he had to fight someone! Nevertheless, the presence in Holland of political exiles and refugees, most outstanding of whom was the future Whig bishop, Gilbert Burnet,[1] disturbed James. Even more alarming was the presence of those six English regiments, many of whose troops were staunch Protestants. Once Monmouth had gone, William and his wife were the practical alternatives to monarchy in England. It was an option which belonged to the future, and William had no desire to force events.

In the spring of 1687 William asked Everard van Weede Dijkveld, his envoy in England, to take soundings on how strong was the opposition to James. He also had to bear in mind how far his own countrymen would welcome his intervention in English affairs. By no means every Dutchman wanted to see William become more powerful and so involve their nation in the larger issues of European politics, whether it was constructing a European alliance against France or acquiring the throne of England to make such an alliance even stronger. For William as ruler in England would weaken Dutch republicanism, heighten French hostility and arouse Imperial jealousy. To those in England who sought his reaction to James's religious policy, he replied, through the propaganda of the pamphlet writer Gaspar Fagel, that he was a man of tolerance but of Protestant sympathies. To those in the Empire who wondered how he would treat the English Catholics he answered that he would pursue a policy of liberty of conscience.[2] To those in his own country he later[3] gave the assurance that it was not his aim to drive James off the throne, but to prevent the prospect of a Franco-English alliance.

Three further factors strengthened William's position in relation to opponents and critics. He was not condemned for his participation in English affairs by the papacy. Innocent XI, a diplomatic and pacific pontiff, had been surprisingly out of sympathy with James's

---

[1] Burnet was a Scots clergymen, an historian and a man of particular value to William, both as an adviser and linguist.

[2] The English Toleration Act of 1689 scarcely met the Emperor Leopold's views on Catholic toleration.

[3] In October 1688.

policies in England, while he was on bad terms with Louis XIV for not crusading against the Turks and for his interference with the Church in France. Secondly the death of the Great Elector, Frederick William, in May 1688 weakened French influence in Germany. Frederick William had had pro-French sympathies, which were not shared by his successor as Elector of Brandenburg, Frederick I. Thirdly, possibly most important, he knew what he was about. His intelligence system was first-rate and no one, in an age that had no technical methods of communication except printing, could have done more than he to have influenced English opinion. His spies were everywhere; letters travelled to Holland constantly; propaganda literature was produced at the staggering rate of 20,000 copies at a time.

It was that crucial month of June 1688 that forced William's hand. Zuylesteen, the man who bore his congratulations to James and Mary of Modena on the birth of James Edward, also brought back the information that responsible men would immediately invite William to England. They did. Danby, ready once more for public office, Henry Compton, suspended bishop of London, and five others told William they would 'not fail to attend his landing' if he could 'give assistance sufficient for a relief under these circumstances which have been now represented'.

In a sense these men were lucky to get William as easily as they did. To the English William was seen as the saviour of Anglicanism, ready to come to England for England's sake. They failed to realize that William had been weighing the pros and cons of coming to England from his own point of view. If he came—and the risks were considerable—it was in the interests of Dutch foreign policy rather than English domestic policy. England was a necessary asset in the reduction of French power.

So the die was cast: James spent the late summer making some minor concessions to Anglicanism, and organizing his naval and land forces. William raised troops from those English regiments still in the Netherlands, from Sweden, from Brandenburg, from Germany. Protestant refugees from the ranks of French Huguenots joined the Protestant crusade. Even the elements were Protestant, as south-westerly gales prevented James's navy from harassing the oncoming Armada. William landed at Torbay on 5 November 1688. James slipped away from his kingdom on 11 December 1688. The foreign policy of the absolutist Stuart monarchs and the para-absolutist Oliver Cromwell was over.

James II's own foreign policy does not attract harsh criticism. In personal terms it certainly did not contribute to his downfall. In national terms it was reasonable to stand aside from Louis XIV's German ambitions, and accept the fact that the Dutch, weakened both by continued republican jealousies of the office of stadtholder and by French economic policies, were no longer a threat to English interests. For James himself, his isolationism was a matter of pride, although there was another aspect to it. It meant an absence of English diplomatic representation in countries such as Sweden, where English economic interests had once been importantly represented.

Although there might be something in common between him and Louis—the absolutism of princes—it was not sufficient to establish an identity between them. James disapproved of Louis's bitter intolerance towards Huguenots and admitted England's economic gain when Huguenot exiles crossed the Channel. A revealing remark at the very end of the reign may be quoted in James's defence: 'I appeal to all who are considering (thinking) men and have had experience whether anything can make the nation great and flourishing as liberty of conscience. Some of our neighbours denied it.'

James II, by default, lacked a foreign policy. He neither pursued an aggressive one whose objectives would be attained by victory in war, nor demanded one of appeasement by an attempt to mediate in European affairs. His business belonged to domestic history, yet it must be seen in the context of European contemporary affairs. Indeed, had not events in Europe stood as they did, the English Revolution would not have been accomplished. For it was Louis's ambitions and his hopes of world dominion—Europe and the Indies—which frightened Protestantism and the Empire and allowed William of Orange to form a League. William wanted England in that League. And it was the tales of Huguenot refugees which stimulated Louis's enemies to form such a coalition. The

European setting in 1688 gave William the confidence to over-throw James.

For James aspired to the absolutism of seventeenth-century princes—and not only Catholic ones. He required, as his fore-fathers had done, the subservience of parliament—to be achieved in his case by packing its ranks. Although it was an attitude with which his son-in-law William had some sympathy and which was not without some chance of success, it failed because James saw such a policy as a prerequisite for the restoration of English Catholic-ism. The Scots Catholic John Jameson saw troubles ahead as early as the first month of the king's reign: 'God grant that such a great prosperity be not a forerunner to some adversity.' In France Madame de Maintenon noted that the king went about matters too abruptly.

When James realized he had failed, his departure was immediate. A sympathetic witness in the closing days of his reign noted 'the road filled with spectators on foot with faces of joy, and balconies and windows thronged with loud acclamations'. James was not entirely without friends as he left England, but those near to him, such as his daughter Anne, had deserted him. He was broken-hearted and beaten. Possibly too he was afraid—'if I do not retire, I shall certainly be sent to the Tower and no king ever went out of that place except to his grave.' Plans for the future could be better made in France than in the Tower of London. A year later James still dreamed of being in a position to provide 'for everything that may contribute to the peace and settlement of our kingdoms'. There we must leave him. William had taken over those kingdoms, acting with *de facto* authority—in such matters as orders to shipping and troop-movements—even before James had left them. William had objectives of his own, and the foreign policy he pursued be-longs more properly to the eighteenth century than the seven-tenth. William of Orange may have looked like a Stuart, but his foreign policy was cast in a different mould.

Map 1. Europe in the seventeenth century

Key to battles	1. Lowestoft	5. Dungeness
	2. Southwold Bay	6. Worcester
	3. North Foreland	7. Dunbar
	4. The Downs	8. Fehrbellin

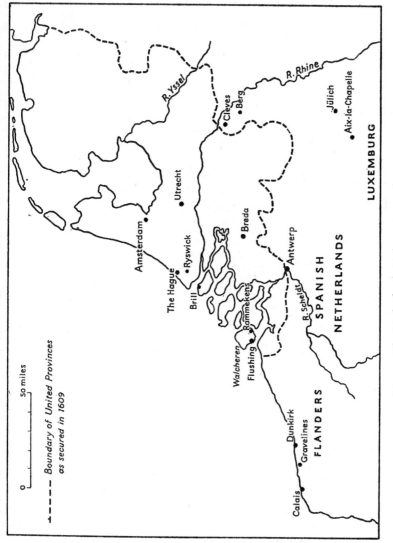

Map 2. The Netherlands in the seventeenth century

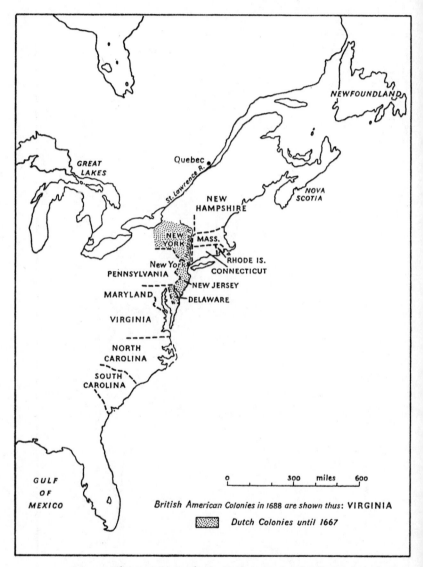

Map 3. The American colonies in the seventeenth century

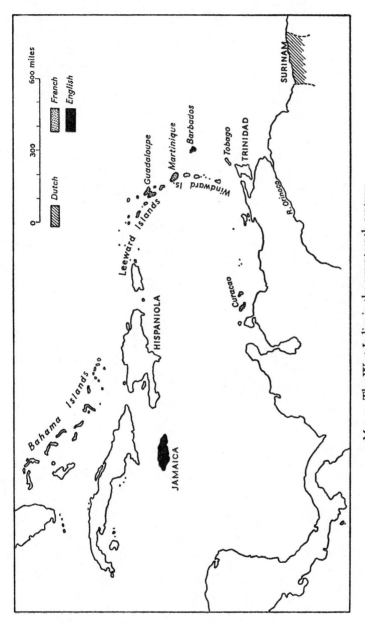

Map 4. The West Indies in the seventeenth century

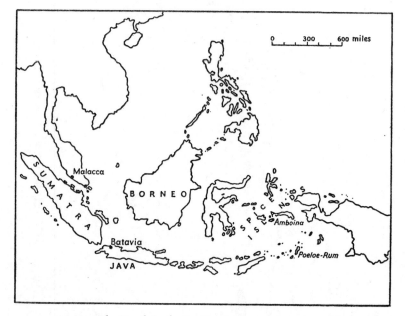

Map 5. The Dutch in the Far East in the seventeenth century

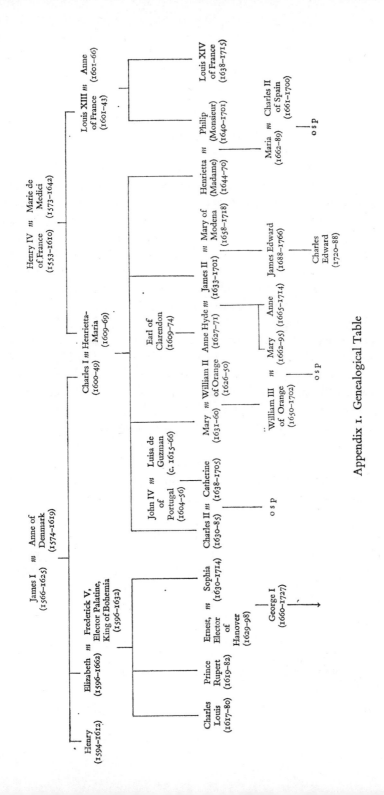

Appendix 1. Genealogical Table

Appendix 2   The peerage

The British peerage involves changes in nomenclature. Apart from possibly changing his name on becoming ennobled, a peer could also change his name by being raised to a higher rank in the peerage. One such peer was the Duke of Leeds (1694), who was the Earl of Danby during the years in which he was important in the later period of Charles II's reign and the whole of James II's. He is never Duke of Leeds within the period covered in this book. In three cases—the Bristol, Buckingham and Southampton peerages—two members of the family are mentioned in the text.

Not all peerages were United Kingdom creations. A Scottish peerage existed until 1707 and an Irish one until 1800. One of Danby's many titles was Viscount Osborne of Dunblane in the Scottish peerage. He first took his seat in the House of Lords as Baron Osborne. Lauderdale was raised to a dukedom and a marquisate in the Scottish peerage in 1672, taking his seat in the House of Lords two years later as a United Kingdom earl.

The list below, in alphabetical order of family name, gives the highest rank in the peerage, with footnotes giving information on other titles, and should be used in conjunction with the index.

FAMILY NAME	HIGHEST RANK IN PEERAGE	DATE
Henry Arundell	Baron Arundell	1643
Francis Bacon	Viscount St. Alban	1621[1]
Henry Bennet	Earl of Arlington	1672[2]
James Butler	Duke of Ormonde	1661[3]
George Calvert	Baron Baltimore	1625
Dudley Carleton	Viscount Dorchester	1628
Robert Carr	Earl of Somerset	1613[4]

[1] Baron Verulam, 1618. The viscountcy is sometimes incorrectly given an 's'.
[2] Baron Arlington, 1665
[3] Earl of Ormonde, 1633; Marquis of Ormonde, 1642.
[4] Viscount Rochester, 1611.

FAMILY NAME	HIGHEST RANK IN PEERAGE	DATE
Edward Cecil	Viscount Wimbledon	1626[5]
Robert Cecil	Earl of Salisbury	1605[6]
William Cecil	Baron Burghley	1571
Thomas Clifford	Baron Clifford	1672
Anthony Ashley Cooper	Earl of Shaftesbury	1672[7]
George Digby	2nd Earl of Bristol	1653
John Digby	1st Earl of Bristol	1622[8]
William Douglas	Duke of Hamilton	1660[9]
John Hay	Marquis of Tweeddale	1694[10]
Robert Jenkinson	Earl of Liverpool	1808
Henry Jermyn	Earl of St. Albans	1660[11]
John Maitland	Duke of Lauderdale	1672[12]
George Monk	Duke of Albemarle	1660
Edward Montagu	Earl of Sandwich	1660
Ralph Montagu	Duke of Montagu	1705[13]
Thomas Osborne	Duke of Leeds	1694[14]
William Pitt	Earl of Chatham	1766
Andrew Rutherford	Earl of Teviot	1663
James Scott	Duke of Monmouth	1663
Robert Spencer	Earl of Sunderland	1643
Richard Talbot	Earl of Tyrconnel	1685[15]
George Villiers	1st Duke of Buckingham	1623[16]
George Villiers	2nd Duke of Buckingham	1628
Robert Walpole	Earl of Orford	1742
Thomas Wentworth	Earl of Strafford	1640[17]
Henry Wriothesley	3rd Earl of Southampton	1581
Thomas Wriothesley	4th Earl of Southampton	1624

[5] Baron Cecil of Putney, 1625.

[6] Baron Cecil, 1603; Viscount Cranborne, 1604.   [7] Baron Ashley, 1661.

[8] Baron Digby, 1618.   [9] Earl of Selkirk, 1646.

[10] Earl of Tweeddale, 1654.   [11] Baron Jermyn, 1643.

[12] Earl of Guildford, 1674.   [13] Earl of Montagu, 1689.

[14] Baron Osborne, 1673; Viscount Latimer, 1673; Earl of Danby, 1674; Marquis of Carmarthen, 1689.

[15] (titular) Duke of Tyrconnel, 1690 (raised in peerage by James II in exile).

[16] Viscount Villiers, 1616; Earl of Buckingham, 1617; Marquis of Buckingham, 1618.   [17] Viscount Wentworth, 1628.

Appendix 3   The secret treaty of Dover, June 1670

1. It is agreed, determined and concluded that there shall be for ever a good, secure and firm peace, union, true fellowship, confederacy, friendship, alliance and good correspondence between the said lord king of Great Britain, his heirs and successors of the one part, and the said most Christian king of the other, and between all and every of their kingdoms, states and territories, as also between their subjects and vassals, that they have or possess at present, or may have, hold and possess hereafter, as well by sea and fresh waters as by land. And as evidence that this peace shall remain inviolable, beyond the capacity of anything in the world to disturb it, there follow articles of so great confidence, and also so advantageous to the said lord kings, that one will hardly find in any age more important provisions determined and concluded.

2. The lord king of Great Britain, being convinced of the truth of the Catholic religion, and resolved to declare it and reconcile himself with the Church of Rome as soon as the welfare of his kingdom will permit, has every reason to hope and expect from the affection and loyalty of his subjects that none of them, even of those upon whom God may not yet have conferred his divine grace so abundantly as to incline them by that august example to turn to the true faith, will ever fail in the obedience that all peoples owe to their sovereigns, even of a different religion. Nevertheless, as there are sometimes mischievous and unquiet spirits who seek to disturb the public peace, especially when they can conceal their wicked designs under the plausible excuse of religion, his Majesty of Great Britain, who has nothing more at heart (after the quiet of his own

conscience) than to confirm the peace which the mildness of his government has gained for his subjects, has concluded that the best means to prevent any alteration in it would be to make himself assured in case of need of the assistance of his most Christian Majesty, who, wishing in this case to give to the lord king of Great Britain unquestionable proof of the reality of his friendship, and to contribute to the success of so glorious a design, and one of such service not merely to his Majesty of Great Britain but also to the whole Catholic religion, has promised and promises to give for that purpose to the said lord king of Great Britain the sum of two million livres tournois, of which half shall be paid three months after the exchange of the ratifications of the present treaty in specie to the order of the said lord king of Great Britain at Calais, Dieppe or Havre de Grace, or remitted by letters of exchange to London at the risk, peril and expense of the said most Christian king, and the other half in the same manner three months later. In addition the said most Christian king binds himself to assist his Majesty of Great Britain in case of need with troops to the number of 6,000 foot-soldiers, and even to raise and maintain them at his own expense, so far as the said lord king of Great Britain finds need of them for the execution of his design; and the said troops shall be transported by ships of the king of Great Britain to such places and ports as he shall consider most convenient for the good of his service, and from the day of their embarkation shall be paid, as agreed, by his most Christian Majesty, and shall obey the orders of the said lord king of Great Britain. And the time of the said declaration of Catholicism is left entirely to the choice of the said lord king of Great Britain.

3. It has also been agreed between the most Christian king and his Majesty of Great Britain that the said most Christian king shall never break or infringe the peace which he has made with Spain, and shall not contravene in any manner what he has promised by the treaty of Aix-la-Chapelle; and consequently it will be possible for the king of Great Britain to maintain the said treaty conformably to the conditions of the Triple Alliance and the engagements that depend upon it.

4. It is also agreed and accepted that if there should hereafter fall to the most Christian king any new titles and rights to the Spanish

monarchy, the said lord king of Great Britain shall assist his most Christian Majesty with all his forces both by sea and land to facilitate the acquisition of the said rights, the whole according to the particular conditions on which the said lord kings propose to agree, as well for the junction of their forces after the maturing of the said titles and rights shall have occurred as for the advantages which the said lord king can reasonably desire. And the said lord kings reciprocally bind themselves from the present moment not to make any treaty on one side or the other because of the said new rights and titles with any prince or potentate whatsoever except by mutual consent and agreement.

5. The said lord kings having each in his own right many more subjects than they would have any need of to justify to the world the resolution they have taken to humble the pride of the States General of the United Provinces of the Low Countries, and to reduce the power of a nation which has so often rendered itself odious by extreme ingratitude to its own founders and the creators of its republic, and which even has the insolence to aim now at setting itself up as sovereign arbiter and judge of all other potentates, it is agreed, decided and concluded that their Majesties will declare and wage war jointly with all their forces by land and sea on the said States General of the United Provinces of the Low Countries, and that neither of the said lord kings will make any treaty of peace, or truce, or suspension of arms with them without the knowledge and consent of the other, as also that all commerce between the subjects of the said lord kings and those of the said States shall be forbidden, and that the vessels and goods of those who carry on trade in defiance of this prohibition may be seized by the subjects of the other lord king, and shall be deemed lawful prize. And all previous treaties made between the said States and either of the said lord kings or their predecessors shall be void, except that of the Triple Alliance made for the maintenance of the treaty of Aix-la-Chapelle. And if after the declaration of war any prisoners are taken from among subjects of either of the said lord kings who shall be enrolled in the service of the said States, or shall at the time be found in it, they shall be put to death by authority of the said lord king whose subjects shall have taken them.

6. And for the purpose of waging and conducting the war as successfully as the said lord kings, in virtue of the justice of their common cause, expect, it is also agreed that his most Christian Majesty will undertake all the expense necessary for setting on foot, maintaining and supporting the operations of the armies required for delivering a powerful attack by land on the strongholds and territory of the said States, the said lord king of Great Britain binding himself only to contribute to the army of the said most Christian king, and to maintain there at his own expense, a body of 6,000 infantry, whose commanding officer shall hold the rank of general, and obey his most Christian Majesty and the supreme commander of the army in which the said body of troops shall serve as auxiliaries. That body shall be composed of six regiments of ten companies each, with a hundred men to each company, and the said troops shall be transported and landed at such ports and harbours, and at such times, as shall be agreed upon hereafter between the said lord kings, in such manner, nevertheless, that they may arrive on the coast of Picardy, or such other place as shall be arranged, one month at latest after the fleets shall unite in the neighbourhood of Portsmouth, as is appointed below.

7. As to what concerns the war at sea, the said lord king of Great Britain shall undertake that burden, and shall fit out at least fifty great ships and ten fire-ships, to which the said most Christian king shall bind himself to add a squadron of thirty good French vessels, of which the smallest shall carry forty pieces of cannon, and a sufficient number of fire-ships, even up to ten if necessary, according to the proportion which there ought to be in the fleet. This auxiliary squadron of French vessels shall continue to serve throughout the period of the said war at the charge and expense of his most Christian Majesty, and in the event of loss of men and vessels they shall be replaced as soon as possible by his most Christian Majesty; and the said squadron shall be commanded by a French vice-admiral or lieutenant-general, who shall obey the orders of his Royal Highness the duke of York in virtue of the powers which the said lord kings shall give to the said lord duke, each for the vessels which belong to him. And if the said lord duke shall attack and engage the Dutch vessels, and do all which he considers most proper for the good of

M

the common cause, he shall enjoy also the honour of the flag, salutes, and all the other authorities, prerogatives and pe-eminences which admirals are accustomed to enjoy; and on the other side also the said French vice-admiral or lieutenant-general shall have for himself precedence in the councils, and for his ship and vice-admiral's flag precedence in sailing, over the English vice-admiral and ship of the same rank. In addition the captains, commanders, officers, sailors and soldiers of each nation shall behave as friends among themselves according to the agreement to be made hereafter, so that no incident may arise which may alter the good union. And in order that the said lord king of Great Britain may more easily support the expense of the war, his most Christian Majesty binds himself to pay to the said king each year that the said war shall last the sum of three millions of livres tournois in the aforesaid manner, of which the first payment, which shall be of 750,000 livres tournois, shall be made three months before the declaration of the war, the second of like sum at the time of the said declaration, and the remainder, amounting to 1,500,000 livres tournois six months after the said declaration. And in the years following, the first payment, which shall be of 750,000 livres tournois, shall be made on the 1st of February, the second of like sum on the 1st of May, and the third, amounting to 1,500,000 livres tournois, on the 15th of October; which sums shall be paid in specie to the order of the king of Great Britain at Calais, Dieppe or Havre de Grace, or else remitted by letters of exchange to London at the risk, peril and expense of the said most Christian king. It is also agreed and determined that the said lord king of Great Britain shall not be bound to declare this war until the auxiliary French squadron of the said thirty vessels and ten fire-ships shall have effected a junction with the English fleet in the neighbourhood of Portsmouth. And of all the conquests which shall be made from the States General his Majesty of Great Britain shall be content with the following places, viz., the island of Walcheren, Sluys, with the island of Cadsand; and the method of attack and the manner of continuing the war shall be regulated by a settlement which shall be agreed upon hereafter. And inasmuch as the dissolution of the government of the States General might involve some prejudice to the prince of Orange, nephew of the king of

Great Britain, and also that some fortresses, towns and governments which belong to him are included in the proposed division of the country, it has been determined and concluded that the said lord kings shall do all they can to secure that the said prince may find his advantage in the continuation and end of the war, as shall hereafter be provided in separate articles.

8. It has also been agreed that before the declaration of war the said lord kings shall do their utmost, jointly or severally as the occasion shall require, to persuade the kings of Sweden and Denmark, or one of them, to enter into this war against the States General, or at least to oblige them to remain neutral; and an attempt will likewise be made to secure the participation of the electors of Cologne and Brandenburg, the House of Brunswick, the duke of Neuburg and the bishop of Münster. The said lord kings shall also do their utmost to persuade even the Emperor and the crown of Spain not to oppose the conquest of the said country.

9. It is likewise agreed and accepted that after the said lord king of Great Britain shall have made the declaration specified in the second article of this treaty, which it is hoped by the grace of God will be followed with good success, it will be entirely within the power and discretion of the said most Christian king to determine the time when the said lord kings shall make war with their united forces against the States General, his Majesty of Great Britain promising to make his declaration of war conjointly at the time that his most Christian Majesty shall judge the most proper for that purpose, the said lord king of Great Britain being assured that his most Christian Majesty in naming the said time will have regard to the interests of the two crowns, which after the conclusion of this treaty will be common to both and inseparable.

10. If in any previous treaty made by one or other of the said lord kings with any prince or state whatever there should be found conditions inconsistent with those specified in this alliance, the said conditions shall be void, and those which are included in the present treaty shall remain in full force and vigour.

And for the better union of the minds and interests of the subjects of the said lord kings, it has been agreed that the treaty of commerce at present being made shall be concluded as soon as possible.

Appendix 4   Time-chart

1603   James I's accession
1604   Treaty of London
1605   Dutch took Amboina
1608   Palatinate entered Protestant Union
1609   Catholic League formed
        Twelve Years Truce
1610   Henry IV assassinated
1612   Death of Prince Henry
1613   Elector Frederick married Princess Elizabeth
        English annexation of Spitzbergen islands
1616   Dutch redeemed the 'cautionary towns'
1617   Ferdinand crowned king of Bohemia
1618   Defenestration of Prague
        Outbreak of Thirty Years War
        Sir Walter Raleigh executed
1619   Ferdinand elected Holy Roman Emperor
        Frederick elected king of Bohemia (August)
        Frederick crowned king of Bohemia (November)
1620   Battle of the White Mountain
1623   Prince Charles in Spain
        Massacre of Amboina
1624   Anglo-Dutch treaty
1625   Anglo-Danish treaty
        Charles I's accession
        Treaty of Southampton
        Treaty of The Hague
        England at war with Spain

1626	Franco-Spanish peace
1627	England at war with France
1628	Buckingham assassinated
	Dutch captured Spanish treasure-fleet
1629	Treaty of Susa
1630	Treaty of Madrid
1632	Death of Frederick
1635	Anglo-Spanish treaty
	Peace of Prague
1637	Siege of Breda
1639	Battle of the Downs
1640	Portuguese and Catalonian revolts
1641	William II of Orange married Princess Mary
	Strafford executed
1642	Outbreak of English Civil War
1648	Treaty of Westphalia
1649	Lower Palatinate restored to Elector Charles Louis
	Charles I executed
1651	English Navigation Act
1652	Outbreak of First Anglo-Dutch War
	Battle of Dungeness
1653	Battle of Portland
	Battle of the Gabbard
	Tromp killed
	Cromwell became Lord Protector
1654	Treaty of Westminster
	Anglo-Swedish treaty
	Anglo-Danish treaty
	Anglo-Portuguese treaty
1655	Capture of Jamaica
	Anglo-French treaty
	Jews readmitted to England
1656	English captured Spanish treasure-fleet
1657	English East India Company became permanent joint-stock
1658	Treaty of Roskilde
	Battle of the Dunes
	Dunkirk handed to English

1658   Death of Cromwell
1659   Peace of the Pyrenees
1660   Charles II's accession
       English Navigation Act
1661   Madame married Philip of Orleans
1662   Charles II married Catherine of Braganza
       Dunkirk sold to France
       Franco–Dutch treaty
1663   Battle of Amegial
1664   English acquired New Netherland
1665   Outbreak of Second Anglo–Dutch War
       Battle of Lowestoft
       Anglo–Swedish treaty
1666   French entered Anglo–Dutch War
       Four-Day Battle
1667   Anglo–Spanish treaty
       Treaty of Breda
1668   Triple Alliance
       Peace of Aix-la-Chapelle
1670   Secret treaty of Dover (June)
       Treaty *simulé* (December)
1672   Outbreak of Third Anglo–Dutch War
       Battle of Southwold Bay
1674   Peace of Westminster
1677   William III of Orange married Princess Mary
1678   Treaty of Nymegen
1684   Truce of Ratisbon
1685   James II's accession
       Monmouth's rebellion
1688   William III landed in England
       James II left England

Bibliography

The books listed below should be reasonably obtainable. Almost all are still in print. I have given the date of original publication: in several cases later editions have appeared. Lengthy lists can be found at the back of the two volumes* in the 'Oxford History of England' which cover the seventeenth century.

Reference should also be made to John Roach, *A Bibliography of Modern History*, 1968, which relates to the *New Cambridge Modern History*, and to Mary Keeler, *Bibliography of British History: Stuart period*, 1970.

The Dictionary of National Biography, 1885, remains a fundamental reference source on the lives and careers of British people. Its mini-counterpart, the *Concise Dictionary of National Biography*, 1903 and many editions since, is also valuable for a straightforward *curriculum vitae* of its subjects. Details of people and events in the seventeenth century may be found in G. M. D. Howat (ed.), *Dictionary of World History*, 1973.

Among periodicals whose indices should be consulted for articles in the period are: *Economic History Review*, *History*, *History Today*, *Journal of Modern History*, *Transactions of the Royal Historical Society*, together with the various publications of the Historical Association.

Maurice Ashley, *Commercial and Financial Policies under the Cromwellian Protectorate*, 1934.
Maurice Ashley, *England in the Seventeenth Century*, 1952.
Maurice Ashley, *The Greatness of Oliver Cromwell*, 1959.
Maurice Ashley, *Charles II*, 1971.
R. Bagwell, *Ireland under the Stuarts*, 1936.

Sir Ernest Barker, *Oliver Cromwell and the English people*, 1937.

Corelli Barnett, *Britain and her Army, 1509–1970*, 1970.

S. B. Baxter, *William III*, 1966.

A. Browning, *Thomas Osborne, Earl of Danby*, 1951.

A. Browning (ed.), *English Historical Documents 1660–1714*, 1953.

Sir Arthur Bryant, *King Charles II*, 1931.

Sir Arthur Bryant, *The Letters of Charles II*, 1935.

Sir Arthur Bryant, *Samuel Pepys: the Man in the Making*, 1933.

Sir Arthur Bryant, *Samuel Pepys: the Years of Peril*, 1935.

Sir Arthur Bryant, *Samuel Pepys: the Saviour of the Navy*, 1938.

John Carswell, *The Descent on England*, 1969.

Sir George Clark, *The Seventeenth Century*, 1929.

*Sir George Clark, *The Later Stuarts*, 1934.

*G. Davies, *The Early Stuarts*, 1937.

G. Davies, *Essays on the Later Stuarts*, 1958.

I. Deane Jones, *The English Revolution, 1603–1714*, 1931.

D. L. Farmer, *Britain and the Stuarts*, 1965.

Sir Keith Feiling, *History of the Tory Party, 1640–1714*, 1924.

Sir Keith Feiling, *British Foreign Policy, 1660–72*, 1930.

Sir Charles Firth, *Oliver Cromwell*, 1900.

M. A. Gibb, *Buckingham*, 1935.

K. D. H. Haley, *The First Earl of Shaftesbury*, 1968.

C. H. Hartmann, *Charles II and Madame*, 1934.

C. H. Hartmann, *Clifford of the Cabal*, 1937.

C. H. Hartmann, *The King My Brother*, 1954.

Christopher Hibbert, *Charles I*, 1968.

Christopher Hill, *The Century of Revolution*, 1961.

Christopher Hill, *God's Englishman: Oliver Cromwell and the English Revolution*, 1970.

A. A. Hillary, *Oliver Cromwell and the Challenge to the English Monarchy*, 1969.

J. R. Jones, *Britain and Europe in the Seventeenth Century*, 1966.

J. R. Jones, *The Revolution of 1688 in England*, 1972.

W. K. Jordan, *The Development of Religious Toleration in England*, 1938.

Betty Kemp, *Kings and Commons, 1660–1832*, 1957.

J. P. Kenyon, *The Stuarts*, 1958.

J. P. Kenyon, *The Stuart Constitution*, 1966.

Maurice Lee, *The Cabal*, 1965.

David Mathew, *James I*, 1967.

William McElwie, *The Wisest Fool in Christendom*, 1958.

D. Ogg, *England in the Reign of Charles II*, 1934.

D. Ogg, *England in the Reigns of James II and William III*, 1955.

J. R. Powell, *Robert Blake*, 1972.

G. S. Pryde, *Scotland from 1603 to the Present Day*, 1962.

M. M. Reese, *The Tudors and Stuarts*, 1940.

P. G. Rogers, *The Dutch in the Medway*, 1970.

A. S. Turberville, *Commonwealth and Restoration*, 1928.

F. C. Turner, *James II*, 1948.

Henri and Barbara van der Zee, *William and Mary*, 1973.

C. V. Wedgwood, *Oliver Cromwell*, 1939.

C. V. Wedgwood, *The King's Peace*, 1955.

C. V. Wedgwood, *The King's War*, 1958.

D. H. Willson, *King James VI and I*, 1956.

Charles Wilson, *Profit and Power: A Study of England in the Dutch Wars*, 1957.

J. B. Wolf, *Louis XIV*, 1968.

N

Index